South Carolina Tract Society

The Soldier's Hymn-Book

South Carolina Tract Society

The Soldier's Hymn-Book

ISBN/EAN: 9783337146658

Printed in Europe, USA, Canada, Australia, Japan

Cover: Foto ©ninafisch / pixelio.de

More available books at **www.hansebooks.com**

THE

SOLDIER'S

HYMN BOOK.

Second Edition (30,000) revised.

CHARLESTON, S. C.
PUBLISHED BY THE SOUTH CAROLINA TRACT SOCIETY.
1863.

CONTENTS

	PAGES
WORSHIP	13—40
THE LORD'S DAY	41—43
THE BIBLE	44—47
MORNING AND EVENING	48—56
THE SAVIOUR	57—85
THE SINNER	86-110
THE CHRISTIAN	111-130
SORROW AND SICKNESS	131-145
DYING AND DEATH	146-166
HEAVEN	167-195

OUR COUNTRY IN WAR—
    Praise and Thanksgiving ... 196-209
    Confidence and Hope ... 210-227
    Prayer, Confession, and Humiliation. 228-243
    Prayer and Thanksgiving for Peace. 244-247
    Sailors ... 248-256

INDEX.

	PAGE
Afflicted land, to Christ draw near	223
Affliction is a stormy deep	135
Alas! and did my Saviour bleed	108
All hail the power of Jesus' name	58
Am I a soldier of the cross	112
An alien from God, and a stranger to grace.	184
And is there, Lord, a rest	191
And will the God of grace	235
Another day of soldier life	53
Approach, my soul, the mercy-seat	89
Arise, ye saints, arise	218
Asleep in Jesus! blessed sleep	157
Assembled in thy name, O Lord	16
Awake, and sing the song	71
Awake my soul, and with the sun	50
Awake, my soul, in joyful lays	62
Awake, our souls! away our fears	116
Before Jehovah's awful throne	195
Begone, unbelief! my Saviour is near	118
Behold us, Lord, and let our cry	244
Beneath the cross of Jesus	115
Be not dismayed, thou little flock	212
Blest Comforter Divine	18
Blest be that voice now heard afar	254

Index.

	PAGE.
By whom was David taught	119
Call Jehovah thy salvation	227
Children of the heavenly King	27
Come, every pious heart	63
Come, holy Spirit! come	17
Come, holy Spirit, heavenly Dove	18
Come, let us join our cheerful songs	59
Come, let us join our friends above	35
Come, Lord, and warm each languid heart	169
Come, my fond, fluttering heart	97
Come, my Redeemer, come	64
Come, my soul, thy suit prepare	14
Come, thou Almighty King	30
Come, thou Fount of every blessing	22
Come to Jesus! come to Jesus	87
Come, trembling sinner, in whose breast	107
Come, ye disconsolate, where'er ye languish	98
Come, ye who love the Lord	24
Daughter of Zion, awake from thy sadness	204
Death shall not destroy my comfort	186
Delay not, delay not; O sinner! draw near	102
Didst thou, dear Jesus, suffer shame	120
Dread Jehovah! God of nations	237
Dread Sovereign, let my evening song	53
Earth has engrossed my love too long	79
Faint not, Christian! though the road	137
Farewell, my dear brethren, the time is at hand	163
Far from these narrow scenes of night	192
Father of all! we bow to thee	36
Father of mercies, in thy word	48
Father, whate'er of earthly bliss	131
Fear not, O little flock, tho foe	211

	PAGE.
Firm and unmoved are they	225
Frequent the day of God returns	42
From stern oppression's haughty land	196
For ever with the Lord	174
Gently, Lord! O gently lead us	147
Give me the wings of faith to rise	182
Give thanks to God most high	199
Give to the winds thy fears	123
Glory to God on high	73
Glory to thee, my God, this night	51
God bless our native land	232
God imposes not a burden	124
God is our refuge in distress	217
God is the refuge of his saints	45
God moves in a mysterious way	220
God of the brave and free	200
God shall charge his angel legions	229
Go to dark Gethsemane	145
Grace! 't is a charming sound	105
Gracious Lord, incline thine ear	106
Great God, inspire each heart and tongue	246
Great Ruler of the earth and skies	245
Guide me, O thou great Jehovah	146
Had not the God of truth and love	226
Hail! sweetest, dearest tie that binds	170
Hallelujah! victory! victory	197
Hark, my soul! it is the Lord	66
Here at thy cross, incarnate God	214
High in yonder realms of light	168
How are thy servants blessed, O Lord	250
How calm and beautiful the morn	41
How firm a foundation, ye saints of the Lord	110
How happy are they	113

Index.

	PAGE.
How long has God bestowed his care	229
How precious is the book divine	46
How sad our state by nature is	89
How sweet, how heavenly is the sight	126
How sweet the name of Jesus sounds	58
How sweet the songs of Zion sound	255
I have fought the good fight, I have finished my race	165
I heard the voice of Jesus say	94
I'll praise my Maker with my breath	39
I love the volume of thy word	47
I love to steal a while away	26
I'm a pilgrim, and I'm a stranger	173
I'm not ashamed to own my Lord	113
I'm weary of straying—O fain would I rest	177
In all my Lord's appointed ways	125
In evil long I took delight	90
Infinite loveliness is thine	77
In thee, great God! with songs of praise	206
In thy great name, O Lord, we come	16
I would not live alway! I ask not to stay	158
In Zion God is known	219
Jerusalem, my happy home	179
Jesus, and shall it ever be	60
Jesus! I come to thee	109
Jesus, I love thy charming name	75
Jesus lives, and so shall I	171
Jesus, lover of my soul	65
Jesus, mine all, to heaven is gone	91
Jesus, my sorrow lies too deep	138
Jesus, Saviour, sympathize	134
Jesus shall reign where'er the sun	61
Jesus, thou everlasting King	72

	PAGE.
Jesus, thy boundless love to me	74
Jesus, who knows full well	241
Joyfully, joyfully, onward I move	175
Just as I am, without one plea	103
Just as thou art, without one trace	104
Kindly the Lord appeared	139
Let me be with Thee where Thou art	172
Look down, O Lord, with pitying eye	245
Lord, I cannot let thee go	23
Lord, I hear of showers of blessing	101
Lord, in the morning thou shalt hear	49
Lord, it belongs not to my care	161
Lord, look on all assembled here	241
Lord, thou hast scourged our bleeding land.	240
Lord, thou wilt hear me when I pray	56
Lord, we come before thee now	29
Lord, when we bow before thy throne	30
Lord, while for all mankind we pray	230
Majestic sweetness sits enthroned	78
Mercy and judgment are my song	228
'Mid scenes of confusion and creature complaints	25
Mourn for the thousands slain	242
My comrades all, on you I call	121
My country! O my country	236
My country, 't is of thee	198
My days are gliding swiftly by	148
My God! I know that I must die	160
My God, my Father, while I stray	133
My God, permit me not to be	19
My God! thy service well demands	140
My God, the spring of all my joys	136
My Jesus, as Thou wilt	131

Index.

	PAGE.
My Saviour, my Almighty Friend	82
My soul, be on thy guard	129
My spirit looks to God alone	221
Not unto us, O Lord	208
Now begin the heavenly theme	76
Now, in a song of grateful praise	79
Now may the God of power and grace	223
Now the shades of night are gone	48
O faint and feeble hearted	127
O for a faith that will not shrink	153
O for an overcoming faith	150
O God of Bethel, by whose hand	221
O holy Saviour! Friend unseen	67
O Lord, another day is flown	54
O Lord of Hosts, to Thee we kneel	233
O Lord, our fathers oft have told	197
O Lord, our languid souls inspire	32
O my soul, what means this sadness	143
O sing to me of heaven	194
O thou in whom thy saints are one	38
O thou, from whom all goodness flows	151
O thou, my light, my life, my joy	33
Oft in sorrow, oft in woe	128
Oh! bless the Lord, my soul	33
Oh! could I speak the matchless worth	57
Oh! for a closer walk with God	38
Oh! for the death of those	154
Oh! haste away, my brethren dear	188
Oh! where shall rest be found	92
One sweetly solemn thought	149
One there is, above all others	70
On Jordan's stormy banks I stand	180
On thee, O Lord our God, we call	243

Index.

	PAGE
Our dearly cherished land	23
Our heavenly Father, hear	1
Our land, O Lord, with songs of praise	20
Our land, with mercies crowned	210
Our sins, alas! how strong they be	165
Plunged in a gulf of dark despair	84
Praised be the Lord of might	2
Prayer was appointed to convey	2
Prepare me, gracious God	155
Prostrate, O Jesus, at thy feet	96
Rejoice—the Lord is King	85
Rock of Ages, cleft for me	95
Safely through another week	43
Saviour, breathe an evening blessing	52
Saviour, thy love alone can fill	141
See, gracious God, before thy throne	231
See the healing fountain springing	100
Shepherd of the ransomed flock	81
Sing of Jesus, sing for ever	75
Sleep not, soldier of the cross	117
Snatched, Lord, from danger and from death	205
Soldiers, by our Lord's command	193
Soldiers of the cross, arise	130
Sovereign of all the worlds above	202
Stand up, my soul, shake off thy fears	114
Sun of my soul! Thou Saviour dear	55
Sweet the moments, rich in blessing	28
The billows swell, the winds are high	248
The Christian warrior—see him stand	126
The Lord appears our helper now	209
The Lord's my banner! forth I go	216
The Lord's my Shepherd, I'll not want	83
The man is ever blest	44

Index. 11

	PAGE.
The Spirit breathes upon the word	45
The voice of free grace cries, " Escape to the mountain"	87
There is a fountain filled with blood	86
There is a happy land	167
There is a land of pure delight	181
There is an hour of peaceful rest	176
Thine earthly Sabbaths, Lord, we love	247
Thou dear Redeemer, dying Lamb	183
Though hard the winds are blowing	253
Though troubles assail and dangers affright.	34
Thy mighty arm, O God, was nigh	207
T is by the faith of joys to come	129
T is faith supports my feeble soul	213
To God I cried with mournful voice	224
To praise our Shepherd's care	80
Toss'd upon life's raging billow	251
To Thee our fathers, Lord, repaired	234
To the hills I lift mine eyes	215
To thine almighty arm we owe	203
We lift our hearts to thee	50
We 'll sing of Christ, no matter who	67
We 're travelling-home to heaven above	99
What various hinderances we meet	15
When Abrah'm, full of sacred awe	243
When along life's thorny road	152
When shall we meet again	190
When I can trust my all with God	142
When in this world of grief and pain	184
When languor and disease invade	139
When many a tempest blew	253
When marshalled on the nightly plain	249
When o'er the mighty deep we rode	256

PAGE.
When rising from the bed of death........159.
When sins and fears prevailing rise 70
When struggling on the bed of pain 144
When through the torn sail the wild tempest
    is streaming 252
When the shaded pilgrim land............187
When the soul, on wings upsoaring........163
When the spark of life is waning..........162
When this passing world is done..........122
When thou, my righteous judge, shalt come.106
When waves of sorrow round me swell.....148
When we pass through yonder river.......173
Whence do our mournful thoughts arise ...222
Where high the heavenly temple stands.... 20
While life prolongs its precious light 93
While, Lord, our souls thy grace adore 238
While wandering to and fro 68
Why do we mourn departing friends 156
Why should we start and fear to die.......154
Will that not joyful be..................178
With grateful hearts, with joyful tongues ..207

HYMNS.

S. M.

1 Our heavenly Father, hear
 The prayer we offer now:
Thy name be hallowed far and near;
 To thee all nations bow!

2 Thy kingdom come, thy will
 On earth be done in love,
As saints and seraphim fulfil
 Thy perfect law above.

3 Our daily bread supply,
 While by thy word we live;
The guilt of our iniquity
 Forgive, as we forgive.

4 From dark temptation's power,
 From Satan's wiles defend;
Deliver in the evil hour,
 And guide us to the end!

5 Thine, then, for ever be
 Glory and power divine;
The sceptre, throne, and majesty
 Of heaven and earth are thine!

2.   7s.

1 Come, my soul, thy suit prepare,
Jesus loves to answer prayer;
He himself has bid thee pray,
Therefore will not say thee nay.

2 Thou art coming to a King,
Large petitions with thee bring;
For his grace and power are such
None can ever ask too much.

3 With my burden I begin—
Lord, remove this load of sin;
Let thy blood, for sinners spilt,
Set my conscience free from guilt.

4 Lord, I come to thee for rest,
Take possession of my breast;
There thy blood-bought right maintain
And without a rival reign.

5 While I am a pilgrim here,
Let thy love my spirit cheer;
As my Guide, my Guard, my Friend,
Lead me to my journey's end.

6 Show me what I have to do,
Every hour my strength renew;
Let me live a life of faith,
Let me die thy people's death.

L. M.

What various hinderances we meet,
In coming to a mercy seat?
Yet who that knows the worth of prayer
But wishes to be often there?

Prayer makes the darkened cloud with-
　draw,
Prayer climbs the ladder Jacob saw,
Gives exercise to faith and love,
Brings every blessing from above.

Restraining prayer, we cease to fight;
Prayer makes the Christian's armor
　bright;
And Satan trembles when he sees
The weakest saint upon his knees.

Have you no words? Ah! think again;
Words flow apace when you complain,
And fill your fellow-creature's ear
With the sad tale of all your care.

Were half the breath thus vainly spent
To heaven in supplication sent,
Your cheerful songs would oftener be,
Hear what the Lord has done for me."

4. L. M.

1 ASSEMBLED in thy name, O Lord,
We plead the promise of thy word;
We gather now to seek thy face—
Oh! may thy presence fill the place.

2 When 'mid the sad, forsaken band
Of thy disciples thou didst stand,
Thy voice, divinely speaking "Peace,"
Bade doubt, and fear, and sorrow cease.

3 Now may we hear the voice of love
Speak peace and pardon from above;
Sweet intercourse with Jesus find,
And prove him powerful, faithful, kind.

4 Oh! send us not away unbless'd,
For on thy gracious word we rest;
We, sinners, to our Saviour flee,
Helpless and hopeless but in thee.

5. C. M.

1 IN thy great name, O Lord, we come
To worship at thy feet;
Oh! pour thy Holy Spirit down
On all that now shall meet.

2 We come to hear Jehovah speak,
To hear the Saviour's voice;
Thy face and favor, Lord, we seek;
Now make our hearts rejoice.

Worship. 17

3 Teach us to pray and praise — to hear
    And understand thy word;
  To feel thy blissful presence near,
    And trust our living Lord.

4 Let sinners now thy goodness prove,
    And saints rejoice in thee;
  Let rebels be subdued by love,
    And to the Saviour flee.

6.   S. M.

1 Come, holy Spirit! come,
    Let thy bright beams arise;
  Dispel the sorrow from our minds,
    The darkness from our eyes.

2 Convince us of our sin,
    Then lead to Jesus' blood;
  And to our wondering view reveal
    The secret love of God.

3 'T is thine to cleanse the heart,
    To sanctify the soul,
  To pour fresh life in every part,
    And new create the whole.

4 Revive our drooping faith;
    Our doubts and fears remove;
  And kindle in our breast the flame
    Of never dying love.

7. S. M.

1 Blest Comforter Divine,
    Whose rays of heavenly love,
Amid our gloom and darkness shine,
    And point our souls above;

2 Thou, who with " still, small voice "
    Dost stop the sinner's way,
And bid the mourning saint rejoice,
    Though earthly joys decay;

3 Thou, whose inspiring breath
    Can make the cloud of care,
And e'en the gloomy vale of death,
    A smile of glory wear;

4 Thou, who dost fill the heart
    With love to all our race,
Blest Comforter! to us impart
    The blessings of thy grace.

8. C. M.

1 Come, Holy Spirit, heavenly Dove,
    With all thy quickening powers;
Kindle a flame of sacred love
    In these cold hearts of ours.

2 Look, how we grovel here below,
    Fond of these trifling toys!
Our souls can neither fly nor go
    To reach eternal joys.

Worship. 19

3 In vain we tune our formal songs;
   In vain we strive to rise—
Hosannas languish on our tongues,
   And our devotion dies.

4 Dear Lord! and shall we ever live
   At this poor, dying rate?
Our love so faint, so cold to thee,
   And thine to us so great.

5 Come, Holy Spirit, heavenly Dove,
   With all thy quickening powers;
Come, shed abroad a Saviour's love,
   And that shall kindle ours.

L. M.

My God, permit me not to be
A stranger to myself and thee;
Amid a thousand thoughts I rove,
Forgetful of my highest love.

Why should my passions mix with earth,
And thus debase my heavenly birth;
Why should I cleave to things below,
And let my God, my Saviour go?

Call me away from flesh and sense,
One sovereign word can draw me thence;
I would obey the voice divine,
And all inferior joys resign.

4 Be earth with all her scenes withdrawn
Let noise and vanity be gone:
In secret silence of the mind,
My heaven, and there my God, I find.

10. L. M.

1 WHERE high the heavenly temple stands
The house of God not made with hands
A great High Priest our nature wears—
The Guardian of mankind appears.

2 Though now ascended up on high,
He bends on earth a brother's eye;
Partaker of the human name,
He knows the frailty of our frame.

3 Our Fellow-sufferer yet retains
A fellow-feeling of our pains;
And still remembers, in the skies,
His tears, his agonies, and cries.

4 In every pang that rends the heart
The Man of sorrows had a part;
He sympathizes in our grief,
And to the sufferer sends relief.

5 With boldness, therefore, at the throne
Let us make all our sorrows known;
And ask the aid of heavenly power,
To help us in the evil hour.

Worship. 21

1.   L. M.
PRAYER was appointed to convey
  The blessings God designs to give;
Long as they live should Christians pray,
  For only while they pray they live.

The Christian's heart his prayer indites,
  He speaks as prompted from within;
The Spirit his petition writes,
  And Christ receives and gives it in.

And wilt thou in dead silence lie,
  When Christ stands waiting for thy prayer?
My soul, thou hast a Friend on high;
  Arise and try thy interest there.

4 If pains afflict or wrongs oppress,
  If cares distract or fears dismay;
If guilt deject, if sin distress,
  The remedy's before thee—Pray.

5 'T is prayer supports the soul that's weak,
  Though thoughts be broken, language lame;
Pray if thou canst or canst not speak;
  But pray with faith in Jesus' name.

6 Depend on Him—thou canst not fail;
  Make all thy wants and wishes known;
Fear not—His merits must prevail;
  Ask what thou wilt, it shall be done.

Worship.

12.   8s and 7s.

1 Come, thou Fount of every blessing,
   Tune my heart to sing thy grace;
Streams of mercy never ceasing,
   Call for songs of loudest praise.
Teach me some melodious sonnet,
   Sung by flaming tongues above;
Praise the mount — Oh! fix me on it,
   Mount of God's unchanging love.

2 Here I raise my Ebenezer,
   Hither by thy help I 'm come;
And I hope by thy good pleasure
   Safely to arrive at home.
Jesus sought me when a stranger,
   Wandering from the fold of God;
He, to rescue me from danger,
   Interposed with precious blood.

3 Oh! to grace how great a debtor
   Daily I 'm constrained to be!
Let that grace, Lord, like a fetter,
   Bind my wandering heart to thee.
Prone to wander, Lord, I feel it;
   Prone to leave the God I love;
Here 's my heart, Lord, take and seal it,
   Seal it from thy courts above.

Worship.

7s.

1 Lord, I cannot let thee go,
Till a blessing thou bestow;
Do not turn away thy face,
Mine 's an urgent, pressing case.

2 Dost thou ask me who I am?
Ah! my Lord, thou knowest my name;
Yet the question gives a plea
To support my suit with thee.

3 Thou didst once a wretch behold
In rebellion blindly bold
Scorn thy grace, thy power defy;
That poor rebel, Lord, was I.

4 Once a sinner, near despair,
Sought thy mercy-seat by prayer;
Mercy heard, and set him free;
Lord, that mercy came to me.

5 Many days have passed since then
Many changes I have seen;
Yet have been upheld till now—
Who could hold me up but thou?

6 Thou hast helped in every need;
This emboldens me to plead—
After so much mercy past,
Canst thou let me sink at last?

7 No, I must maintain my hold,
  'T is thy goodness makes me bold;
  I can no denial take,
  When I plead for Jesus' sake.

14.   S. M.

1 Come, ye who love the Lord!
  And let your joys be known;
  Join in a song of sweet accord,
  And thus surround the throne.

2 Let those refuse to sing
  Who never knew our God;
  But children of the heavenly King
  May speak their joys abroad.

3 The men of grace have found
  Glory begun below;
  Celestial fruits on earthly ground
  From faith and hope may grow.

4 The hill of Zion yields
  A thousand sacred sweets
  Before we reach the heavenly fields
  Or walk the golden streets.

5 Then let our songs abound,
  And every tear be dry;
  We 're marching through Immanuel'
    ground,
  To fairer worlds on high.

Worship.

5. 11s.

1 'Mid scenes of confusion and creature complaints
How sweet to my soul is communion with saints;
To find at the banquet of mercy there's room,
And feel in the presence of Jesus at home!

2 Sweet bonds, that unite all the children of peace;
And thrice precious Jesus, whose love cannot cease;
Though oft from thy presence in sadness I roam,
I long to behold thee, in glory, at home.

3 I sigh from this body of sin to be free,
Which hinders my joy and communion with thee;
Though now my temptations like billows may foam,
All, all will be peace, when I'm with thee at home.

4 While here in the valley of conflict I stay,
O give my submission and strength as my day;
In all my afflictions, to thee I would come,
Rejoicing in hope of my glorious home.

5 What'er thou deniest, O give me thy grace,
The Spirit's sure witness, and smiles of thy face;
Inspire me with patience to wait at thy throne,
And find, even now, a sweet foretaste of home.

6 I long, dearest Lord, in thy beauties to shine,
No more as an exile in sorrow to pine;
And in thy dear image arise from the tomb,
With glorified millions to praise thee at home.

16. C. M.

1 I LOVE to steal awhile away
From every cumbering care,
And spend the hours of setting day
In humble, grateful prayer.

2 I love in solitude to shed
The penitential tear,
And all his promises to plead
Where none but God can hear.

3 I love to think on mercies past,
And future good implore;
And all my cares and sorrows cast
On Him whom I adore.

Worship.

4 I love by faith to take a view
   Of brighter scenes in heaven;
   The prospect does my strength renew,
   While here by tempests driven.

5 Thus, when life's toilsome day is o'er,
   May its departing ray
   Be calm as this impressive hour,
   And lead to endless day.

17. 7s.

1 CHILDREN of the heavenly King!
   As ye journey, sweetly sing;
   Sing your Saviour's worthy praise,
   Glorious in his works and ways.

2 Ye are travelling home to God
   In the way the fathers trod;
   They are happy now, and ye
   Soon their happiness shall see.

3 Shout, ye little flock! and blest
   You on Jesus' throne shall rest;
   There your seat is now prepared—
   There your kingdom and reward.

4 Fear not, brethren! joyful stand
   On the borders of your land;
   Jesus Christ, your Father's Son,
   Bids you undismayed go on.

5 Lord! submissive make us go,
   Gladly leaving all below;
Only thou our leader be,
   And we still will follow thee.

18.   8s and 7s.

1 Sweet the moments, rich in blessing,
   Which before the Cross I spend,
Life, and health, and peace possessing,
   From the sinner's dying Friend.

2 Love and grief my heart dividing,
   With my tears his feet I'll bathe;
Constant still in faith abiding,
   Life deriving from his death.

3 Here I'll sit forever viewing
   Mercy flow in streams of blood;
Precious drops, my soul bedewing,
   Plead and claim my peace with God.

4 Truly blessed is this station,
   As before his Cross I lie,
And behold divine compassion
   Beaming from his pitying eye.

5 Here it is I find my heaven,
   While upon the Cross I gaze—
Love I much? I'm much forgiven;
   I'm a miracle of grace.

19.   7s.

1 Lord, we come before thee now,
At thy feet we humbly bow;
O, do not our suit disdain—
Shall we seek thee, Lord, in vain?

2 Lord, on thee our souls depend;
In compassion now descend;
Fill our hearts with thy rich grace,
Tune our lips to sing thy praise.

3 In thine own appointed way,
Now we seek thee, here we stay;
Lord, we know not how to go
Till a blessing thou bestow.

4 Send some message from thy word
That may joy and peace afford;
Let thy spirit now impart
Full salvation to each heart.

5 Comfort those who weep and mourn,
Let the time of joy return;
Those who are cast down, lift up,
Make them strong in faith and hope.

6 Grant that all may seek, and find
Thee a God supremely kind:
'Heal the sick, the captive free;
Let us all rejoice in thee.

20. C. M.

1 Lord, when we bow before thy throne,
   And our confessions pour,
Oh, may we feel the sins we own,
   And hate what we deplore.

2 Our contrite spirits, pitying, see;
   True penitence impart;
And let a healing ray from thee
   Beam hope on every heart.

3 When we disclose our wants in prayer,
   Oh, let our wills resign,
And not a thought our bosom share
   Which is not wholly thine.

4 Let faith each meek petition fill,
   And waft it to the skies,
And teach our hearts 't is goodness still,
   That grants it, or denies.

21. 6s and 4s.

1 Come, thou Almighty King,
   Help us thy name to sing,
     Help us to praise!
Father all glorious,
O'er all victorious,
Come and reign over us,
   Ancient of days.

Worship.

2 Jesus, our Lord, arise,
Scatter our enemies,
  And make them fall!
Let thine almighty aid
Our sure defence be made;
Our souls on thee be stay'd;
  Lord, hear our call!

3 Come, thou, incarnate Word,
Gird on thy mighty sword;
  Our prayer attend!
Come, and thy people bless,
And give our cause success;
Spirit of holiness,
  On us descend!

4 Come, holy comforter,
Thy sacred witness bear,
  In this glad hour;
Thou, who almighty art,
Now rule in ev'ry heart,
And ne'er from us depart,
  Spirit of power.

5 To thee, great ONE IN THREE,
The highest praises be,
  Hence evermore!
Thy sovereign majesty,
May we in glory see,
And to eternity
  Love and adore!

22. C. M.

1 O Lord, our languid souls inspire,
  For here, we trust, thou art;
Kindle a flame of heavenly fire,
  In every waiting heart.

2 Dear Shepherd of thy people, hear;
  Thy presence now display;
As thou hast given a place for prayer,
  So give us hearts to pray.

3 Show us some token of thy love,
  Our fainting hope to raise;
And pour thy blessing from above,
  That we may render praise.

4 Within our hearts let holy peace,
  And love and concord dwell;
And give the troubled conscience ease,
  The wounded spirit heal.

5 The feeling heart, the melting eye,
  The humbled mind bestow;
And shine upon us from on high,
  To make our graces grow.

6 May we in faith receive thy word,
  In faith present our prayers;
And in the presence of our Lord
  Unbosom all our cares.

Worship.

3. S. M.

Oh! bless the Lord, my soul,
 Let all within me join,
And aid my tongue to bless his name;
 Whose favors are divine.

Oh! bless the Lord my soul,
 Nor let his mercies lie
Forgotten in unthankfulness,
 And without praises die.

'T is he forgives thy sins,
 'T is he relieves thy pain,
'T is he that heals thy sicknesses,
 And makes thee young again.

He crowns thy life with love,
 When ransomed from the grave;
He that redeemed my soul from hell
 Hath sovereign power to save.

He fills the poor with good,
 He gives the sufferers rest;
The Lord hath judgments for the proud,
 And justice for th' oppressed.

4. C. M.

1 O Thou, my light, my life, my joy,
 My glory and my all!
Unsent by thee, no good can come,
 Nor evil can befall.

2 Such are thy schemes of providence,
 And methods of thy grace,
That I may safely trust in thee,
 Through all the wilderness.
3 'Tis thine outstretched and powerful a[rm]
 Upholds me in the way;
And thy rich bounty well supplies
 The wants of every day.
4 For such compassion, O my God!
 Ten thousand thanks are due;
For such compassion, I esteem
 Ten thousand thanks too few.

25.   10s and 11s.

1 Though troubles assail and dang[er]
 affright;
Though friends should all fail, and f[oes]
 all unite;
Yet one thing secures us, whatever b[e]
 tide:
The scriptures assure us the Lord w[ill]
 provide.
2 His call we obey, like Abram of old,
 Not knowing our way, but faith makes [us]
 bold;
For though we are strangers we have [a]
 good guide,
And trust in all dangers the Lord w[ill]
 provide.

Worship.

When Satan appears to stop up our path,
And fills us with fears, we triumph by
  faith;
He cannot take from us, though oft he
  has tried,
This heart-cheering promise — the Lord
  will provide.

He tells us we're weak, our hope is in
  vain,
The good that we seek we ne'er shall
  obtain;
But where such suggestions our spirits
  have plied
This answers all questions—the Lord will
  provide.

When life sinks apace, and death is in
  view
This word of his grace shall comfort us
  through;
No fearing or doubting, with Christ on
  our side,
We hope to die shouting the Lord will
  provide.

6.   C. M.

1 COME, let us join our friends above
  That have obtained the prize;
And on the eagle wings of love
  To joy celestial rise.

2 Let saints below his praises sing
    With those to glory gone;
  For all the servants of our King
    In heaven and earth are one.

3 One family, we dwell in him,
    One church above, beneath;
  Though now divided by the stream,
    The narrow stream of death.

4 One army of the living God,
    To his commands we bow;
  Part of the host have crossed the flood
    And part are crossing now.

5 How many to their endless home
    This solemn moment fly;
  And we are to the margin come,
    And soon expect to die.

6 Dear Saviour be our constant guide;
    Then when the word is given,
  Bid the cold waves of death divide,
    And land us safe in heaven.

27.   C. M.

1 FATHER of all! we bow to thee,
    Who art in heaven adored;
  But present still through all thy works
    The universal Lord.

Worship.

Forever hallowed be thy name,
   By all beneath the skies;
And may thy kingdom still advance,
   Till grace to glory rise.

A grateful homage may we yield,
   With hearts resigned to thee;
And as in heaven thy will is done,
   On earth so let it be.

From day to day we humbly own
   The hand that feeds us still;
Give us our bread, teach us to rest
   Contented in thy will.

Our sins before thee we confess—
   Oh! may they be forgiven;
As we to others mercy show,
   We mercy beg from heaven.

Still let thy grace our life direct,
   From evil guard our way;
And in temptation's fatal path
   Permit us not to stray.

For thine the power, the kingdom thine,
   All glory's due to thee;
Thine from eternity they were,
   And thine shall ever be.

28.   C. M.

1 O THOU, in whom thy saints are one,
  Permit us now to see,
In this short hour of prayer and praise
  A glimpse of heaven and thee.

2 While with one heart and one desire,
  Low at thy feet we kneel,
Oh! warm our hearts with heavenly love
  And all thy grace reveal.

3 Thy gracious presence, Lord, alone
  Can make our worship blest;
Drive from our thoughts a vexing world
  And lay our griefs to rest.

4 Descend, and bless our waiting souls,
  And meet us as thine own;
And fit us to ascend and praise
  Before th' eternal throne.

29.   C. M.

1 Oh! for a closer walk with God,
  A calm and heavenly frame—
A light to shine upon the road
  That leads me to the Lamb!

2 Where is the blessedness I knew,
  When first I saw the Lord?
Where is the soul-refreshing view
  Of Jesus and his word?

Worship.

3 What peaceful hours I once enjoyed!
 How sweet their mem'ry still!
But they have left an aching void
 The world can never fill.

4 Return, O holy Dove! return,
 Sweet messenger of rest!
I hate the sins that made thee mourn,
 And drove thee from my breast.

5 The dearest idol I have known,
 What'er that idol be,
Help me to tear it from thy throne,
 And worship only thee.

6 So shall my walk be close with God,
 Calm and serene my frame;
So purer light shall mark the road
 That leads me to the Lamb.

0.   C. M.—6 *line.*

I 'LL praise my Maker with my breath,
And when my voice is lost in death
 Praise shall employ my nobler powers;
My days of praise shall ne'er be past,
While life, and thought, and being last,
 Or immortality endures.

2 Why should I make a man my trust?
　Princes must die, and turn to dust:
　　Vain is the help of flesh and blood;
　Their breath departs, their pomp, and
　　　power,
　And thoughts all vanish in an hour;
　　Nor can they make their promise good.

3 Happy the man whose hopes rely
　On Israel's God; He made the sky,
　　And earth, and seas, with all their train
　His truth for ever stands secure;
　He saves th' oppressed, he feeds the poor:
　　And none shall find his promise vain.

4 The Lord hath eyes to give the blind;
　The Lord supports the sinking mind;
　　He sends the lab'ring conscience peace
　He helps the stranger in distress,
　The widow and the fatherless,
　　And grants the pris'ner sweet release.

5 He loves his saints, he knows them well,
　But turns the wicked down to hell;
　　Thy God, O Zion, ever reigns;
　Let ev'ry tongue, let ev'ry age,
　In this exalted work engage:
　　Praise him in everlasting strains.

The Lord's Day. 41

6 I'll praise him while he lends me breath;
And, when my voice is lost in death,
   Praise shall employ my nobler powers:
My days of praise shall ne'er be past,
While life, and thought, and being last,
   Or immortality endures.

31.   C. L. M.

1 How calm and beautiful the morn
   That gilds the sacred tomb,
Where once the Crucified was borne,
   And veiled in midnight gloom!
O weep no more the Saviour slain;
The Lord is risen—He lives again.

2 Ye mourning saints, dry every tear
   For your departed Lord;
"Behold the place—He is not here,"
   The tomb is all unbarred;
The gates of death were closed in vain;
The Lord is risen—He lives again.

3 Now cheerful to the place of prayer,
   Our early footsteps bend;
The Saviour will himself be there—
   Our Advocate and Friend:
Once by the law our hopes were slain,
But now in Christ we live again.

The Lord's Day.

4 How tranquil now the rising day!
   'T is Jesus still appears,
A risen Lord to chase away
   Our unbelieving fears:
O weep no more our comforts slain;
The Lord is risen — He lives again.

6 And when the shades of evening fall,
   When life's last hour draws nigh,
If Jesus shines upon the soul,
   How blissful then to die!
Since He has risen who once was slain
We die in Christ to live again.

32.   C. M.

1 FREQUENT the day of God returns
   To shed its quickening beams;
And yet, how slow devotion burns!
   How languid are its flames!

2 Accept our faint attempts to love;
   Our follies, Lord forgive;
We would be like thy saints above,
   And praise thee while we live.

3 Increase, O Lord, our faith and hope,
   And fit us to ascend
Where the assembly ne'er breaks up,
   And Sabbaths never end—

The Lord's Day. 43

4 Where we shall breath in heavenly air,
  With heavenly lustre shine;
Before the throne of God appear,
  And feast on love divine.

5 There shall we join, and never tire
  To sing immortal lays;
And, with the bright, seraphic choir,
  Sound forth Immanuel's praise.

33. 7s.

1 SAFELY through another week
    God has brought us on our way;
  Let us now a blessing seek,
    Waiting in his courts to-day;
  Day of all the week the best,
  Emblem of Eternal rest.

2 While we seek supplies of grace,
    Through the dear Redeemer's name;
  Show thy reconciling face,
    Take away our sin and shame;
  From our worldly cares set free,
  May we rest this day in thee.

3 May the gospel's joyful sound
    Conquer sinners, comfort saints,
  Make the fruits of grace abound,
    Bring relief from all complaints:
  Thus let all our Sabbaths prove,
  Till we join the church above.

34. S. M.

1 The man is ever blest,
   Who shuns the sinner's ways,
Among their councils never stands,
   Nor takes the scorner's place—

2 But makes the law of God
   His study and delight,
Amid the labors of the day,
   And watches of the night.

3 He like a tree shall thrive,
   With waters near the root;
Fresh as the leaf his name shall live;
   His works are heavenly fruit.

4 Not so th' ungodly race;
   They no such blessings find;
Their hopes shall flee like empty chaff
   Before the driving wind.

5 How will they bear to stand
   Before that judgment seat,
Where all the saints at Christ's right hand
   In full assembly meet?

6 God knows, and he approves
   The way the righteous go;
But sinners and their works shall meet
   A dreadful overthrow.

The Bible. 45

35. C. M.

1 THE Spirit breathes upon the word,
   And brings the truth to sight;
Precepts and promises afford
   A sanctifying light.

2 A glory gilds the sacred page,
   Majestic like the sun;
It gives a light to every age,
   It gives — but borrows none.

3 The hand that gave it still supplies
   The gracious light and heat;
His truths upon the nations rise—
   They rise, but never set.

4 Let everlasting thanks be thine,
   For such a bright display,
As makes a world of darkness shine,
   With beams of heavenly day.

5 My soul rejoices to pursue
   The steps of him I love,
Till glory breaks upon my view,
   In brighter worlds above.

36. L. M.

1 GOD is the refuge of his saints,
   When storms of sharp distress invade;
Ere we can offer our complaints,
   Behold him present with his aid.

2 Let mountains from their seats be hurled,
   Down to the deep and buried there—
Convulsions shake the solid world,
   Our faith shall never yield to fear.

3 Loud may the troubled ocean roar—
   In sacred peace our souls abide;
While ev'ry nation, ev'ry shore,
   Trembles and dreads the swelling tide.

4 There is a stream, whose gentle flow
   Supplies the city of our God;
Life, love, and joy still gliding through,
   And wat'ring our divine abode.

5 That sacred stream, thy holy word,
   Our grief allays, our fear controls;
Sweet peace thy promises afford,
   And give new strength to fainting souls.

6 Zion enjoys her monarch's love,
   Secure against a threat'ning hour;
Nor can her firm foundations move,
   Built on his truth, and armed with power.

37. C. M.

1 How precious is the book divine,
   By inspiration given!
Bright as a lamp its doctrines shine,
   To guide our souls to heaven.

The Bible. 47

2 It sweetly cheers our drooping hearts,
  In this dark vale of tears;
Life, light, and joy it still imparts,
  And quells our rising fears.
3 This lamp, through all the tedious night
  Of life, shall guide our way;
Till we behold the clearer light
  Of an eternal day.

38.   C. M.—6 *line.*

1 I LOVE the volume of thy word;
What light and joy those leaves afford
  To souls benighted and distressed!
Thy precepts guide my doubtful way,
Thy fear forbids my feet to stray,
  Thy promise leads my heart to rest.
2 Thy threatenings wake my slumbering eyes,
And warn me where my danger lies;
  But 't is thy blessed gospel, Lord,
That makes my guilty conscience clean,
Converts my soul, subdues my sin,
  And gives a free, but large reward.
3 Who knows the errors of his thoughts?
My God! forgive my secret faults,
  And from presumptuous sins restrain:
Accept my poor attempts of praise,
That I have read thy book of grace,
  And book of nature not in vain.

39. C. M.

1 Father of mercies, in thy word
What endless glory shines!
Forever be thy name adored
For these celestial lines.

2 Here my Redeemer's welcome voice
Spreads heavenly peace around;
And life and everlasting joys
Attend the blissful sound.

3 Oh! may these heavenly pages be
My ever dear delight;
And still new beauties may I see,
And still increasing light;

4 Divine Instructor, gracious Lord,
Be thou forever near;
Teach me to love thy sacred word,
And view my Saviour there.

40. 7s.

1 Now the shades of night are gone;
Now the morning light is come;
Lord, may we be thine to-day,
Drive the shades of sin away.

2 Fill our souls with heavenly light,
Banish doubt and gloomy night;
In thy service, Lord, to-day,
Help us labor, help us pray.

Morning and Evening. 49

3 Keep our haughty passions bound;
 Save us from our foes around;
 Going out, and coming in,
 Keep us safe from every sin.

4 When our work of life is past,
 O receive us then at last!
 Night of sin will be no more,
 When we reach the heavenly shore.

41.   C. M.

1 Lord, in the morning thou shalt hear
  My voice ascending high;
 To thee will I direct my prayer,
  To thee lift up mine eye.

2 Up to the hills where Christ is gone,
  To plead for all his saints,
 Presenting at his father's throne
  Our songs and our complaints.

3 Thou art a God, before whose sight
  The wicked shall not stand;
 Sinners shall ne'er be thy delight,
  Nor dwell at thy right hand.

4 O may thy Spirit guide my feet,
  In ways of righteousness;
 Make ev'ry path of duty straight,
  And plain before my face.

42.   L. M.

1 Awake my soul, and with the sun
Thy daily course of duty run;
Shake off dull sloth, and early rise
To pay thy morning sacrifice.

2 Lord, I my vows to thee renew,
Scatter my sins as morning dew;
Guard my first springs of thought and
    will,
And with thyself my spirit fill.

3 Direct, control, suggest this day,
All I design, or do, or say;
That all my powers, with all my might,
In thy sole glory may unite.

4 All praise to thee who safe hast kept,
And hast refreshed me while I slept;
Grant, Lord, when I from death shall
    wake,
I may of endless life partake.

43.   S. M.

1 We lift our hearts to thee,
    Thou Day-star from on high;
The sun itself is but thy shade,
    Yet cheers both earth and sky.

2 Oh, let thy rising beams
   Dispel the shades of night:
   And let the glories of thy love
   Come like the morning light!

3 How beauteous nature now!
   How dark and sad before!
   With joy we view the pleasing change,
   And nature's God adore.

4 May we this life improve,
   To mourn for errors past;
   And live this short, revolving day
   As if it were our last.

44. L. M.

1 GLORY to thee, my God, this night,
For all the blessings of the light:
Keep me, oh, keep me, King of kings!
Beneath the shadow of thy wings.

2 Forgive me, Lord! through thy dear Son,
The ill which I this day have done;
That with the world, myself, and thee,
I, ere I sleep, at peace may be.

3 Teach me to live, that I may dread
The grave as little as my bed;
Teach me to die, that so I may
Rise glorious at thy judgment day.

4 Be thou my guardian while I sleep,
Thy watchful station near me keep;
My heart with love celestial fill,
And guard me from th' approach of ill.

5 Lord, let my soul forever share
The bliss of thy paternal care!
'T is heaven on earth, 't is heaven above
To see thy face, and sing thy love.

6 Praise God, from whom all blessings flow
Praise him, all creatures here below;
Praise him above, ye heavenly host;
Praise Father, Son, and holy Ghost.

45. 8s and 7s.

1 SAVIOUR, breathe an evening blessing,
  Ere repose our spirits seal:
Sin and want we come confessing;
  Thou canst save, and thou canst heal

2 Though destruction walk around us,
  Though the arrow near us fly,
Angel guards from thee surround us;
  We are safe, if thou art nigh.

3 Though the night be dark and dreary,
  Darkness cannot hide from thee:
Thou art He who, never weary,
  Watcheth where thy people be.

Morning and Evening.

Should swift death this night o'ertake us,
  And our couch become our tomb,
May the morn in heaven awake us,
  Clad in light and deathless bloom!

46.   C. M.

1 ANOTHER day of soldier life
  Is numbered with the past;
It was not filled with bloody strife,
  And did not prove our last.

2 Thy grace, O God, hath kept us whole;
  To thee we lift our praise;
Accept the homage of each soul,
  And keep us all our days.

3 Keep us in safety through the night,
  And with us those we love;
Save us, we pray thee, by thy might,
  To reign with thee above.

47.   C. M.

1 DREAD Sovereign, let my evening song
  Like holy incense rise:
Assist the offerings of my tongue,
  To reach the lofty skies.

2 Through all the dangers of the day,
  Thy hand was still my guard:
And still to drive my wants away
  Thy mercy stood prepared.

3 Perpetual blessings from above,
Encompassed me around:
But O how few returns of love
Has my Creator found!

4 What have I done for Him who died
To save my wretched soul?
How are my follies multiplied,
Fast as my minutes roll!

5 Lord, with this guilty heart of mine,
To thy dear cross I flee;
And to thy grace my soul resign,
To be renewed by thee.

48. C. M.

1 O Lord, another day is flown,
And we, a little band,
Are met once more before thy throne
To bless thy fostering hand.

2 And wilt thou bend a listening ear,
To praises low as ours?
Thou wilt, for thou dost deign to hear
The song that meekness pours.

3 And, Jesus, thou thy smiles wilt deign,
As we before thee pray;
For thou didst bless the infant train,
And we are less than they.

Morning and Evening.

4 Oh! let thy grace perform its part;
   Let sin's dominion cease;
And shed abroad in every heart,
   Thine everlasting peace.

49.   L. M.

1 SUN of my soul! Thou Saviour dear,
It is not night if thou be near:
O may no earth-born cloud arise
To hide thee from thy servant's eyes.

2 When the soft dews of kindly sleep
My wearied eyelids gently steep,
Be my last thought, how sweet to rest
Forever on my Saviour's breast.

3 Abide with me from morn till eve,
For without thee I cannot live:
Abide with me when night is nigh,
For without thee I dare not die.

4 Watch by the sick; enrich the poor
With blessings from thy boundless store
Be every mourner's sleep to-night
Like infants' slumbers, pure and light.

5 Come near and bless us when we wake
 Ere through the world our way we tak
 Till in the ocean of thy love,
 We lose ourselves, in heaven above.

50. C. M.

1 Lord, thou wilt hear me when I pray
   I am forever thine:
 I fear before thee all the day,
   Nor would I dare to sin.

2 And while I rest my weary head
   From cares and business free,
 'T is sweet conversing on my bed
   With my own heart and thee.

3 I pay this evening sacrifice;
   And when my work is done,
 Great God, my faith and hope relies
   Upon thy grace alone.

4 Thus, with my thoughts composed peace,
   I 'll give mine eyes to sleep;
 Thy hand in safety keeps my days,
   And will my slumbers keep.

The Saviour.

1.   L. C. M.—6 *line.*

Oh! could I speak the matchless worth,
Oh! could I sound the glories forth
  Which in my Saviour shine!
I'd soar, and touch the heavenly strings,
And vie with Gabriel while he sings,
  In notes almost divine.

I'd sing the precious blood he spilt,
My ransom from the dreadful guilt
  Of sin and wrath divine:
I'd sing his glorious righteousness,
In which all perfect, heavenly dress,
  My soul shall ever shine.

3 I'd sing the characters he bears,
And all the forms of love he wears,
  Exalted on his throne:
In loftiest songs of sweetest praise,
I would to everlasting days
  Make all his glories known.

4 Well, the delightful day will come
When my dear Lord will bring me home,
  And I shall see his face:
Then, with my Saviour, Brother, Friend,
A blest eternity I'll spend,
  Triumphant in his grace.

52. C. M.

1 How sweet the name of Jesus sounds
 In a believer's ear!
It soothes his sorrows, heal his wounds,
 And drives away his fear.

2 It makes the wounded spirit whole,
 And calms the troubled breast;
'T is manna to the hungry soul,
 And to the weary, rest.

3 By him, my prayers acceptance gain,
 Although with sin defiled;
Satan accuses me in vain,
 And I am owned a child.

4 Weak is the effort of my heart,
 And cold my warmest thought;
But when I see thee as thou art,
 I'll praise thee as I ought.

5 Till then I would thy love proclaim,
 With every fleeting breath;
And may the music of thy name
 Refresh my soul in death.

53. C. M.

1 ALL hail the power of Jesus' name!
 Let angels prostrate fall;
Bring forth the royal diadem,
 And crown Him Lord of all.

The Saviour.

2 Ye chosen seed of Israel's race,
   Ye ransomed from the fall,
Hail Him, who saves you by his grace,
   And crown Him Lord of all.

3 Sinners, whose love can ne'er forget
   The wormwood and the gall,
Go, spread your trophies at his feet,
   And crown him Lord of all.

4 Let every kindred, every tribe,
   On this terrestrial ball,
To Him all majesty ascribe,
   And crown Him Lord of all.

5 Oh! that with yonder sacred throng,
   We at his feet may fall;
We'll join the everlasting song,
   And crown Him Lord of all.

54. C. M.

1 COME let us join our cheerful songs,
   With angels round the throne;
Ten thousand thousand are their tongues,
   But all their joys are one.

2 Worthy the Lamb that died, they cry,
   To be exalted thus:
Worthy the Lamb, our lips reply,
   For he was slain for us.

The Saviour.

3 Jesus is worthy to receive
    Honor and Power divine;
And blessings more than we can give
    Be, Lord, for ever thine.

4 Let all who dwell above the sky,
    And air, and earth, and seas,
Conspire to lift thy glories high,
    And speak thine endless praise.

5 The whole creation join in one,
    To bless the sacred name,
Of Him who sits upon the throne,
    And to adore the Lamb.

55. L. M.

1 Jesus! and shall it ever be,
A mortal man ashamed of thee!
Asham'd of thee, whom angels praise,
Whose glories shine through endless days?

2 Asham'd of Jesus! sooner far
Let evening blush to own a star;
He sheds the beams of light divine
O'er this benighted soul of mine.

3 Ashamed of Jesus!—just as soon
Let midnight be asham'd of noon;
'T is midnight with my soul, till He,
Bright morning Star, bid darkness flee.

The Saviour.

Asham'd of Jesus!—that dear Friend
On whom my hopes of heav'n depend?
No! when I blush be this my shame,
That I no more revere His name.

Asham'd of Jesus! yes, I may,
When I 've no guilt to wash away;
No tear to wipe; no good to crave;
No fear to quell—no soul to save.

Till then—nor is my boasting vain—
Till then I boast a Saviour slain!
And Oh! may this my glory be,
That Christ is not asham'd of me.

56. L. M.

1 Jesus shall reign where'er the sun
 Does his successive journeys run;
 His kingdom stretch from shore to shore,
 Till suns shall rise and set no more.

2 To him shall endless prayer be made,
 And endless praises crown his head;
 His name, like sweet perfume, shall rise,
 With every morning sacrifice.

3 People and realms of every tongue
 Dwell on his love with sweetest song;
 And infant voices shall proclaim
 Their early blessings on his name.

4 Let every creature rise and bring
Peculiar honors to our King;
Angels descend with songs again,
And earth repeat the loud Amen.

57. L. M.

1 Awake, my soul, in joyful lays,
And sing thy great Redeemer's praise;
He justly claims a song from thee;
His loving kindness, O how free!

2 He saw me ruined in the fall,
Yet loved me notwithstanding all;
He saved me from my lost estate;
His loving kindness, O how great!

3 Though numerous hosts of mighty foes,
Though earth and hell my way oppose,
He safely leads my soul along,
His loving kindness, O how strong!

4 When trouble, like a gloomy cloud,
Has gathered thick, and thundered loud
He near my soul has always stood;
His loving kindness, O how good!

5 Often I feel my sinful heart,
Prone from my Saviour to depart;
But though I oft have him forgot,
His loving kindness changes not.

The Saviour.

Soon shall I pass the gloomy vale,
Soon all my mortal powers must fail;
Oh! may my last expiring breath,
His loving kindness sing in death.

Then let me mount and soar away,
To the bright world of endless day;
And sing with rapture and surprise,
His loving kindness in the skies.

8.   H. M.

COME, every pious heart
  That loves the Saviour's name,
Your noblest powers exert
  To celebrate his fame:
Tell all above, and all below,
The debt of love to him you owe.

He left his starry crown,
  And laid his robes aside;
On wings of love came down,
  And wept, and bled, and died.
What he endured, oh! who can tell?
To save our souls from death and hell.

From the dark grave he rose,
  The mansion of the dead;
And thence his mighty foes
  In glorious triumph led;
Up thro' the sky the conqueror rode,
And reigns on high, the Saviour God.

4 Jesus, we ne'er can pay
    The debt we owe thy love;
  Yet tell us how we may
    Our gratitude approve:
  Our hearts—our all to thee we give:
  The gift, though small, do thou receive

59.   H. M.

1 Come, my Redeemer, come,
    And deign to dwell with me;
  Come, and thy right assume,
    And bid thy rivals flee:
  Come, my Redeemer, quickly come,
  And make my heart thy lasting home.

2 Exert thy mighty power,
    And banish all my sin;
  In this auspicious hour,
    Bring all thy graces in:
  Come, my Redeemer, quickly come,
  And make my heart thy lasting home.

3 Rule thou in every thought
    And passion of my soul,
  Till all my powers are brought
    Beneath thy full control:
  Come, my Redeemer, quickly come,
  And make my heart thy lastiug home.

The Saviour.

4 Then shall my days be thine,
 And all my heart be love ;
And joy and peace be mine,
 Such as are known above :
Come, my Redeemer, quickly come,
And make my heart thy lasting home.

60.   7s.

1 JESUS, lover of my soul,
 Let me to thy bosom fly,
While the raging billows roll,
 While the tempest still is high.
Hide me, oh! my Saviour, hide,
 Till the storm of life is past;
Safe into the haven guide ;
 Oh! receive my soul at last.

2 Other refuge have I none,
 Hangs my helpless soul on thee ;
Leave, ah! leave me not alone,
 Still support and comfort me ;
All my trust on thee is staid,
 All my help from thee I bring;
Cover my defenceless head,
 With the shadow of thy wing.

3 Thou, oh Christ, art all I want!
 All in all in thee I find ;
Raise the fallen, cheer the faint,
 Heal the sick, and lead the blind.

Just and holy is thy name,
  I am all unrighteousness;
Vile and full of sin I am,
  Thou art full of truth and grace.

61. 7s.

1 Hark, my soul, it is the Lord—
'Tis thy Saviour, hear his word;
Jesus speaks, and speaks to thee:
" Say, poor sinner, lovest thou me?

2 " I delivered thee when bound,
And, when wounded, healed thy wound;
Sought thee wandering, set thee right,
Turned thy darkness into light.

3 " Mine is an unchanging love,
Higher than the heights above;
Deeper than the depths beneath,
Free and faithful, strong as death.

4 " Thou shalt see my glory soon,
When the work of grace is done;
Partner of my throne shalt be;
Say, poor sinner, lovest thou me?"

5 Lord, it is my chief complaint,
That my love is weak and faint:
Yet I love thee and adore,
Oh! for grace to love thee more.

The Saviour.

62. 7s.

1 O HOLY Saviour! Friend unseen!
Since on thy arm thou bid'st us lean,
Help us throughout life's changing scene
    By faith to cling to Thee.

2 Though far from home, fatigued, opprest,
Here we have found a place of rest;
As exiles still, yet not unblest,
    Because we cling to Thee.

3 Though oft we seem to tread alone
Life's dreary waste, with thorns o'ergrown,
Thy voice of love, in gentlest tone,
    Whispers "Still cling to Me!"

4 We fear not Satan, nor the grave,
We know Thee near, and strong to save;
With Thee all danger we can brave,
    Because we cling to Thee.

5 Blest is our lot, whate'er befall;
Who can affright, or who appall;
Since, as our strength, our Rock, our all,
    Jesus, we cling to Thee?

63. C. M.

1 WE 'LL sing of Christ, no matter who
Should disapprove the theme:
When He is precious to our view,
We can't but sing of Him.

The Saviour

2 And He is precious in the sight
   Of all who know His voice:
'T was He who brought them to the
    light,
And taught them to rejoice.

3 'T is He who cheers them by His smile,
   And guards them by His power;
Who keeps them safe from force and
    guile,
In every trying hour.

4 'T is He who will conduct them home,
   Beyond the reach of ill:
Where all his ransomed people come,
Where saints for ever dwell.

5 Then let His people make their boast
   Of Him, and Him alone,
Who came from heaven to save the lost;
The praise be His alone.

64.   6, 3.

1 WHILE wandering to and fro,
   In this wide world of woe,
Where streams of sorrow flow,
    Give me Jesus—give me Jesus—give
      me Jesus—
    You may have all this world—give me
      Jesus.

The Saviour.

2 When tears o'erflow mine eye,
 When pressed by grief I sigh,
 Still this shall be my cry,
   Give me Jesus, etc.

3 When to the mercy seat
 I go my Lord to meet,
 My heart shall still repeat,
   Give me Jesus, etc.

4 And when my faith is tried,
 In him will I confide,
 And all the storms outride—
   Give me Jesus, etc.

5 Though strength and friends should fail,
 And foes my soul assail,
 Through him I shall prevail—
   Give me Jesus, etc.

6 And when my toils are o'er,
 When nearing Jordan's shore,
 I'll shout as up I soar,
   Give me Jesus, etc.

7 When at the judgment seat,
 I stand at Jesus' feet,
 When worlds on worlds shall meet,
   Give me Jesus, etc.

8 When heaven and earth shall flee,
 When time shall cease to be,
 Through all eternity,
   Give me Jesus, etc.

65. L. M.

1 When sins and fears prevailing rise,
  And fainting hope almost expires,
Jesus, to thee I lift mine eyes,
  To thee I breathe my soul's desires.

2 If my immortal Saviour lives,
  Then my eternal life is sure;
His word a firm foundation gives,
  Here I can build and rest secure.

3 Here would my faith unshaken dwell,
  For ever firm the promise stands;
Not all the powers of earth and hell
  Can e'er dissolve the sacred bands.

4 Here, O my soul, thy trust repose;
  If Jesus is forever thine,
Not death itself, that last of foes.
  Shall break a union so divine.

66. 8s and 7s.

1 One there is, above all others,
  Well deserves the name of Friend;
His is love beyond a brother's,
  Costly, free, and knows no end;
They who once his kindness prove,
Find it everlasting love.

The Saviour. 71

2 Which of all our friends, to save us
    Could or would have shed their blood?
But our Jesus died to have us
    Reconciled in him to God:
This is boundless love indeed!
Jesus is a friend in need.

3 When he lived on earth abased,
    Friend of sinners was his name;
Now above all glory raised,
    He rejoices in the same:
Still he calls them brethren, friends,
And to all their wants attends.

4 Oh! for grace our hearts to soften,
    Teach us, Lord, at length to love;
We, alas! forget too often,
    What a Friend we have above:
But when home our souls are brought,
We will love thee as we ought.

67.   S. M.

1 AWAKE, and sing the song
    Of Moses and the Lamb;
Wake every heart and every tongue,
    To praise the Saviour's name.

2 Sing of his dying love,
    Sing of his rising power,
Sing how he intercedes above
    For those whose sins he bore.

3 Sing till we feel our heart
    Ascending with our tongue;
  Sing till the love of sin depart,
    And grace inspire our song.

4 Sing on your heavenly way,
    Ye ransom'd sinners, sing;
  Sing on, rejoicing every day
    In Christ, th' eternal King.

5 Soon shall we hear him say,
    " Ye blessed children, come;"
  Soon will he call us hence away,
    And take his wanderers home.

6 Soon shall our raptured tongue
    His endless praise proclaim;
  And sweeter voices tune the song
    " Of Moses and the Lamb."

68. L. M.

1 Jesus, thou everlasting King,
  Accept the tribute which we bring;
  Accept the well deserved renown,
  And wear our praises as thy crown.

2 Let every act of worship be
  Like our espousals, Lord, to thee;
  Like the dear hour, when from above,
  We first received thy pledge of love.

The gladness of that happy day
Our hearts would wish it long to stay:
Nor let our faith forsake its hold,
Nor comforts sink, nor love grow cold.

Each following minute, as it flies,
Increase thy praise, improve our joys;
Till we are raised to sing thy name
At the great supper of the Lamb.

39.   6s and 4s.

1 GLORY to God on high!
  Let earth and skies reply,
    Praise ye his name;
      His love and grace adore,
      Who all our sorrows bore:
      Sing loud for evermore,
    Worthy the Lamb.

2 Jesus our Lord and God,
  Bore sin's tremendous load,
    Praise ye his name;
      Tell what his arm has done,
      What spoils from death he won:
      Sing his great name alone,
    Worthy the Lamb.

The Saviour.

3 While they around the throne,
  Cheerfully join in one,
    Praising his name;
      Those who have felt his blood
      Sealing their peace with God
      Sound his dear fame abroad,
    Worthy the Lamb.

4 Join, all ye ransomed race,
  Our holy Lord to bless;
    Praise ye his name;
      In him we will rejoice,
      And make a joyful noise,
      Shouting with heart and voice
    Worthy the Lamb.

70. L. M.

1 Jesus, thy boundless love to me
  No thought can reach, no tongue declare;
  Unite my thankful heart to thee,
  And reign without a rival there.

2 Thy love, how cheering is its ray!
  All pain before its presence flies;
  Care, anguish, sorrow, melt away
  Where'er its healing beams arise.

3 Oh! let thy love my soul inflame,
  And to thy service sweetly bind;
  Transfuse it through my inmost frame
  And mould me wholly to thy mind

The Saviour

Thy love, in sufferings, be my peace;
  Thy love, in weakness, make me strong;
And when the storms of life shall cease,
  Thy love shall be in heaven my song.

71.   C. M.

Jesus, I love thy charming name;
  'Tis music to mine ear;
Fain would I sound it out so loud
  That earth and heaven should hear.

2 Yes, thou art precious to my soul,
  My joy, my hope, my trust;
Jewels, to thee, are gaudy toys,
  And gold is sordid dust.

3 Thy grace still dwells upon my heart,
  And sheds its fragrance there;
The noblest balm of all its wounds,
  The cordial of its care.

4 I'll speak the honors of thy name
  With my last laboring breath;
Then speechless clasp thee in mine arms,
  The antidote of death.

72.   8s and 5s.

1 Sing of Jesus, sing for ever
Of the love that changes never:
Who or what from him can sever
  Those he makes his own?

2 With his blood the Lord hath bought
them;
When they knew him not, he sought
them,
And from all their wand'rings brought
them:
His the praise alone.

3 Through the desert Jesus leads them,
With the bread of heaven he feeds them,
And through all the way he speeds them
To their home above.

4 There they see the Lord who bought
them,
Him who came from heaven and sought
them,
Him who by his spirit taught them:
Him they serve and love.

5 Sing of Jesus, sing for ever,
Sing the love that changes never:
Who or what from him can sever
Those he makes his own?

73.   7s.

1 Now begin the heav'nly theme,
Sing aloud in Jesus' name;
Ye who Jesus' kindness prove,
Triumph in redeeming love.

The Saviour.

2 Ye who see the Father's grace,
    Beaming in the Saviour's face,
    As to Canaan on ye move,
    Praise and bless redeeming love.

3 Mourning souls, dry up your tears,
    Banish all your guilty fears;
    See your guilt and curse remove,
    Cancell'd by redeeming love.

4 Ye, alas! who long have been
    Willing slaves of death and sin!
    Now from bliss no longer rove,
    Stop and taste redeeming love.

5 Welcome, all by sin oppress'd—
    Welcome to his sacred rest:
    Nothing brought him from above,
    Nothing—but redeeming love.

4. C. M.

Infinite loveliness is thine,
    Thou blessed Prince of grace!
Thine uncreated beauties shine,
    With never fading rays.

Sinners, from earth's remotest end,
    Come bending at thy feet;
To thee their prayers and vows ascend,
    In thee their wishes meet.

3 Millions of happy spirits live
    On thine exhaustless store;
  From thee they all their bliss receive,
    And still thou givest more.

4 Thou art their triumph and their joy—
    They find their all in thee:
  Thy glories will their tongues employ,
    Through all eternity.

75.   C. M.

1 Majestic sweetness sits enthroned
    Upon the Saviour's brow;
  His head with radiant glories crowned,
    His lips with grace o'erflow.

2 To him I owe my life and breath,
    And all the joys I have:
  He makes me triumph over death,
    And saves me from the grave.

3 To heaven, the place of his abode,
    He brings my weary feet;
  Shows me the glories of my God,
    And makes my joys complete.

4 Since from his bounty I receive
    Such proofs of love divine,
  Had I a thousand hearts to give,
    Lord, they should all be thine.

6.   C. M.

Earth has engrossed my love too long!
  'T is time I lift mine eyes
Upward, dear Father, to thy throne,
  And to my native skies.

Seraphs, with elevated strains,
  Circle the throne around,
And move and charm the starry plains
  With an immortal sound.

Jesus, the Lord, their harps employs,
  Jesus, my love, they sing!
Jesus, the life of both our joys,
  Sounds sweet from every string.

Now let me mount and join their song,
  And be an angel too;
My heart, my hand, my ear, my tongue—
  Here's joyful work for you.

I would begin the music here,
  And so my soul should rise;
O for some heavenly notes to bear
  My passions to the skies!

7.   L. M.

Now in a song of grateful praise,
To my dear Lord my voice I'll raise;
With all his saints I'll join to tell
That Jesus hath done all things well.

2 Wisdom, and power, and love divine,
In all his works, unrivalled, shine,
And force the wondering world to tell
That he alone did all things well.

3 Howe'er mysterious are his ways,
Or dark and sorrowful my days;
And though my spirit oft rebel,
I know he still doth all things well.

4 And when I stand before his throne,
And all his ways are fully known,
This note in sweetest strains shall swell,
That Jesus hath done all things well.

78.   S. M.

1 To praise our Shepherd's care,
   His wisdom, love, and might,
Your loudest, loftiest songs prepare,
   And bid the world unite.

2 Supremely good and great,
   He tends his blood-bought fold;
He stoops, though throned in highest state,
   The feeblest to uphold.

3 He hears their softest plaint;
   He sees them when they roam;
And if his meanest lamb should faint,
   His bosom bears it home.

The Saviour.

Kind Shepherd of the sheep!
  A feeble flock are we;
And snares and foes are nigh; oh keep
  The lambs who look to thee.

And, if through death's dark vale
  Our feet should early tread,
Oh! may we reach thy fold, and hail
  The Love which there hath led!

79.   7s.

1 SHEPHERD of the ransomed flock,
  Lead us to the shadowing rock,
  Where the cooling waters flow,
  Where the freshening pastures grow.

2 Saviour, when thy loved ones stray
  From the new and living way,
  Gently call thine own by name;
  All our wand'ring steps reclaim.

3 Through the hours of darksome night
  Keep us in thy watchful sight;
  O'er each deadly foe prevail;
  Let no harm thy fold assail.

4 Jesus, who thy life didst give,
  Dying that thy sheep might live,
  Let us in thy presence rest,
  With eternal comfort blest.

80.   C. M.

1 My Saviour, my Almighty Friend,
    When I begin thy praise
  Where will the growing numbers end,
    The numbers of thy grace?

2 Thou art my everlasting trust;
    Thy goodness I adore;
  And since I knew thy graces first
    I speak thy glories more.

3 My feet shall travel all the length
    Of the celestial road;
  And march, with courage in thy strength,
    To see my Father, God.

4 When I am fill'd with sore distress
    For some surprising sin,
  I'll plead thy perfect righteousness,
    And mention none but thine.

5 How will my lips rejoice to tell
    The victories of my King!
  My soul, redeem'd from sin and hell,
    Shall thy salvation sing.

6 Awake, awake, my tuneful powers!
    With this delightful song
  I'll entertain the darkest hours,
    Nor think the season long.

81.   C. M.

1 THE Lord's my Shepherd, I'll not want,
    He makes me down to lie
In pastures green : He leadeth me
    The quiet waters by.

2 My soul He doth restore again,
    And me to walk doth make
Within the paths of righteousness,
    Even for his own name's sake.

3 Yea, though I walk in death's dark vale,
    Yet will I fear no ill ;
For thou art with me, and thy rod
    And staff me comfort still.

4 My table thou hast furnished
    In presence of my foes ;
My head thou dost with oil anoint,
    And my cup overflows.

5 Goodness and mercy all my life
    Shall surely follow me :
And in God's house for evermore
    My dwelling place shall be.

82. C. M.

1 Plunged in a gulf of dark despair
    We wretched sinners lay—
Without one cheerful beam of hope,
    Or spark of glimmering day!

2 With pitying eyes the Prince of grace
    Beheld our helpless grief;
He saw—and Oh! amazing love!
    He ran to our relief.

3 Down from the shining seats above
    With joyful haste he fled,
Enter'd the grave in mortal flesh,
    And dwelt among the dead.

4 He spoil'd the powers of darkness thus,
    And brake our iron chains;
Jesus has freed our captive souls
    From everlasting pains.

5 Oh! for this love let rocks and hills
    Their lasting silence break;
And all harmonious human tongues
    The Saviour's praises speak.

The Saviour.

33.   H. M.

1 REJOICE—the Lord is King:
    Your God and King adore;
  Mortals, give thanks and sing,
    And triumph evermore:
  Lift up the heart, lift up the voice,
  Rejoice aloud, ye saints rejoice.

2 Rejoice—the Saviour reigns!
    The God of truth and love;
  When he had purged our stains,
    He took his seat above:
  Lift up the heart, lift up the voice,
  Rejoice aloud, ye saints rejoice.

3 His kingdom cannot fail,
    He rules o'er earth and heaven:
  The keys of death and hell
    Are to our Jesus given:
  Lift up the heart, lift up the voice,
  Rejoice aloud, ye saints rejoice.

4 Rejoice in glorious hope,
    Jesus the Judge shall come—
  And take his servants up
    To their eternal home:
  We soon shall hear the archangel's voice:
  The trump of God shall sound—rejoice!

84. C. M.

1 THERE is a fountain filled with blood
   Drawn from Immanuel's veins,
And sinners plunged beneath that flood
   Lose all their guilty stains.
Chorus—I do believe, I will believe,
   That Jesus died for me,
   That on his cross he shed his blood
   From sin to set me free.

2 The dying thief rejoiced to see
   That fountain in his day;
And there may I, as vile as he,
   Wash all my sins away.—*Chorus.*

3 Dear, dying Lamb, thy precious blood
   Shall never lose its power,
Till all the ransomed Church of God
   Be saved, to sin no more.—*Chorus.*

4 E'er since, by faith, I saw the stream
   Thy flowing wounds supply,
Redeeming love has been my theme,
   And shall be till I die.—*Chorus.*

5 Then in a nobler, sweeter song,
   I'll sing thy power to save;
When this poor lisping, stammering
      tongue
   Lies silent in the grave.—*Chorus.*

The Sinner

85.   C. M.

Come to Jesus! come to Jesus!
  Come to Jesus, just now!
Just now! come to Jesus!
Come to Jesus! come to Jesus!
Come to Jesus! come to Jesus!
Come to Jesus! come to Jesus!
  Just now, just now,
Just now, come to Jesus!
  Come to Jesus, just now!

2 He will save you! He will save you! etc.
3 Only trust him! only trust him! etc.
4 He is able! He is able! etc.
5 He is willing! He is willing! etc.
6 I believe it! I believe it! etc.

86.   12s.

1 The voice of free grace cries, "Escape
    to the mountain:"
  For Adam's lost race Christ hath opened
    a fountain:
  For sin, and uncleanness, and every transgression,
  His blood flows so freely in streams of
    salvation.
Chorus—Hallelujah to the Lamb who has
      bought us a pardon,
    We'll praise him again when we
      pass over Jordan.

2 Ye souls that are wounded, to the Saviour repair,
Now he calls you in mercy—and can you forbear?
Though your sins are increased as high as a mountain,
His blood can remove them—it flows from the fountain.
Chorus.

3 Our Jesus his name now proclaims all victorious,
He reigns over all, and his kingdom is glorious;
To Jesus we'll join with the great congregation,
And triumph, ascribing to him our salvation.
Chorus.

4 With joy shall we stand when escaped to the shore;
With harps in our hands we will praise him the more;
We'll range the sweet plains on the bank of the river,
And sing of salvation for ever and ever.
Chorus.

The Sinner.

87.   C. M.

1 APPROACH, my soul, the mercy-seat,
   Where Jesus answers prayer;
There humbly fall before his feet,
   For none can perish there.

2 Thy promise is my only plea,
   With this I venture nigh;
Thou callest burden'd souls to thee,
   And such, O Lord, am I.

3 Bow'd down beneath a load of sin,
   By Satan sorely press'd,
By war without, and fear within,
   I come to thee for rest.

4. Be thou my shield and hiding place;
   That, shelter'd near thy side,
I may my fierce accuser face,
   And tell him "thou hast died."

5. Oh! wondrous love, to bleed and die,
   To bear the cross and shame,
That guilty sinners, such as I,
   Might plead thy gracious name.

88.   C. M.

1 How sad our state by nature is!
   Our sin, how deep it stains!
And Satan binds our captive minds
   Fast in his slavish chains.

2 But there's a voice of sov'reign grace
    Sounds from the sacred word:
"Ho! ye despairing sinners, come,
    And trust upon the Lord."

3 My soul obeys th' almighty call,
    And runs to this relief;
I would believe thy promise, Lord;
    Oh! help my unbelief.

4 To the dear fountain of thy blood,
    Incarnate God, I fly;
Here let me wash my spotted soul
    From crimes of deepest dye.

5 A guilty, weak, and helpless worm,
    On thy kind arms I fall:
Be thou my strength and righteousness,
    My Jesus and my all.

89.   C. M.

1 In evil long I took delight,
    Unawed by shame or fear,
Till a new object struck my sight,
    And stopped my wild career.

2 I saw One hanging on a tree
    In agonies and blood:
He fixed his languid eyes on me,
    As near his cross I stood.

The Sinner.

3 O never, till my latest breath,
  Shall I forget that look :
It seemed to charge me with his death,
  Though not a word he spoke.

4 My conscience felt and owned the guilt;
  It plunged me in despair;
I saw my sins his blood had spilt,
  And helped to nail him there.

5 A second look he gave, which said:
  "I freely all forgive;
This blood is for thy ransom paid;
  I die that thou may'st live."

6 Thus, while his death my sin displays
  In all its darkest hue,
Such is the mystery of grace,
  It seals my pardon too.

90. L. M.

1 JESUS, mine all, to heaven is gone,
He whom I fix my hopes upon!
His track I see, and I'll pursue
The narrow way till him I view.

2 This is the way I long have sought,
And mourned because I found it not;
My grief and burden long has been,
Because I could not cease from sin.

The Sinner.

3 The more I strove against its power,
I sinned and stumbled but the more;
Till late I heard my Saviour say:
" Come hither, soul, *I am the way.*"

4 Lo! glad I come! and thou, blest Lamb!
Shalt take me to thee as I am;
My sinful self to thee I give:
Nothing but love shall I receive.

5 Then will I tell to sinners round
What a dear Saviour I have found:
I 'll point to thy redeeming blood,
And say—*Behold the way to God!*

91. S. M.

1 Oh! where shall rest be found—
 Rest for the weary soul?
'T were vain the ocean depths to sound,
 Or pierce to either pole.

2 The world can never give
 The bliss for which we sigh;
'T is not the whole of life to live,
 Nor all of death to die.

3 Beyond this vale of tears
 There is a life above;
Unmeasured by the flight of years;
 And all that life is love.

The Sinner.

4 There is a death whose pang
   Outlasts the fleeting breath :
Oh! what eternal horrors hang
   Around the second death!

5 Lord God of truth and grace,
   Teach us that death to shun ;
Lest we be banished from thy face,
   And evermore undone.

92.   L. M.

1 While life prolongs its precious light,
   Mercy is found, and peace is given,
But soon, ah! soon, approaching night
   Shall blot out every hope of heaven.

2 While God invites, how blest the day!
   How sweet the gospel's charming sound!
Come, sinners haste, oh! haste away,
   While yet a pardoning God he 's found.

3 Soon, borne on time's most rapid wing,
   Shall death command you to the grave,
Before his bar your spirits bring,
   And none be found to hear or save.

4 In that lone land of deep despair
   No Sabbath's heavenly light shall rise;
No God regard your bitter prayer,
   Nor Saviour call you to the skies.

5 Now God invites—how blest the day!
  How sweet the gospel's charming sound
Come, sinners haste, oh! haste away,
  While yet a pard'ning God is found.

93. D. C. M.

1 I HEARD the voice of Jesus say,
    Come unto me and rest;
  Lay down, thou weary one, lay down
    Thy head upon my breast.
  I came to Jesus as I was,
    Weary, and worn, and sad,
  I found in Him a resting place,
    And He has made me glad.

2 I heard the voice of Jesus say,
    Behold, I freely give
  The living water; thirsty one,
    Stoop down and drink and live.
  I came to Jesus, and I drank
    Of that life-giving stream;
  My thirst was quenched, my soul revived,
    And now I live in Him.

3 I heard the voice of Jesus say,
    I am this dark world's light,
  Look unto me, thy morn shall rise,
    And all thy days be bright.

The Sinner.

I looked to Jesus, and I found
In him my Star, my Sun;
And in that light of life I'll walk,
Till travelling days are done.

94.   7s.

1 Rock of ages, cleft for me,
Let me hide myself in thee;
Let the water and the blood
From thy wounded side which flowed,
Be of sin the double cure;
Cleanse me from its guilt and power.

2 Not the labor of my hands
Can fulfil the law's demands;
Could my zeal no respite know,
Could my tears forever flow,
All for sin could not atone,
Thou must save, and thou alone.

3 Nothing in my hand I bring,
Simply to thy cross I cling;
Naked, come to thee for dress;
Helpless, look to thee for grace;
Vile, I to the fountain fly,
Wash me, Saviour, or I die.

4 While I draw this fleeting breath,
  When my heart-strings break in death,
  When I soar to worlds unknown,
  See thee on thy judgment throne,
  Rock of ages, cleft for me,
  Let me hide myself in thee.

95.   C. M.

1 PROSTRATE, O Jesus, at thy feet
    A guilty rebel lies,
  And upward to thy mercy-seat
    Presumes to lift his eyes.

2 If tears of sorrow would suffice
    To pay the debt I owe,
  Tears should from both my weeping eyes
    In ceaseless torrents flow.

3 But no such sacrifice I plead
    To expiate my guilt;
  No tears but those which thou hast shed,
    No blood but thou hast spilt.

4 Think of thy sorrows, dearest Lord,
    And all my sins forgive;
  Then justice will approve the word
    That bids the sinner live.

The Sinner.

96. H. M.

1 COME, my fond, fluttering heart!
  Come, struggle to be free;
Thou and the world must part,
  However hard it be:
My trembling spirit owns it just,
But cleaves yet closer to the dust.

2 Ye tempting sweets! forbear;
  Ye dearest idols! fall;
My love ye must not share,
  Jesus shall have it all:
'T is bitter pain—'t is cruel smart—
But, ah! thou must consent, my heart!

3 Ye fair, enchanting throng!
  Ye golden dreams! farewell!
Earth hath prevailed too long,
  And now I break the spell:
Farewell, ye joys of early years!
Jesus! forgive these parting tears.

4 In Gilead there is balm,
  A kind Physician there
My fevered mind to calm,
  And bid me not despair:
Aid me, dear Saviour! set me free;
My all I would resign to thee.

5 Oh! may I feel thy worth,
   And let no idol dare—
No vanity of earth,
   With thee, my Lord! compare:
Now bid all worldly joys depart,
And reign supremely in my heart.

97. 11s and 10s.

1 COME, ye disconsolate, where'er ye lan
   guish :
Come to the mercy-seat, fervently kneel
Here bring your wounded hearts, her
   tell your anguish;
Earth has no sorrow that heaven ca
   not heal.

2 Joy to the desolate, light of the strayin
   Hope of the penitent, fadeless and pu
Here speaks the Comforter, tender
   saying,
Earth has no sorrow that heaven c
   not cure.

3 Here see the bread of life; see wat
   flowing
Forth from the throne of God, p
   from above;
Come to the feast of love; come,
   knowing
Earth has no sorrow heaven ca
   remove.

98. 8s and 6s.

1 WE 'RE travelling home to heaven above,
  Will you go?
To sing the Saviour's dying love,
  Will you go?
Millions have reached the blest abode,
Anointed kings and priests to God,
And millions more are on the road,
  Will you go?

2 We 're going to see the bleeding Lamb,
  Will you go?
In rapturous strains to praise his name,
  Will you go?
The crown of life we there shall wear,
The conqueror's palms our hands shall bear,
And all the joys of heaven we 'll share,
  Will you go?

3 We 're going to join the heavenly choir,
  Will you go?
To raise our voice and tune the lyre,
  Will you go?
There saints and angels gladly sing
Hosanna to their God and King,
And make the heavenly arches ring,
  Will you go?

4 Ye weary, heavy-laden, come,
    Will you go?
In the blest house there still is room,
    Will you go?
The Lord is waiting to receive,
If thou wilt on him now believe
Thy troubled conscience he'll relieve,
    Come, believe.

5 The way to heaven is straight and plain,
    Will you go?
Repent, believe, be born again,
    Will you go?
The Saviour cries aloud to thee,
"Take up thy cross and follow me,
And thou shalt my salvation see,
    Come to me!"

EVEN THEE.
99.   8s and 7s.

1 SEE the healing fountain springing
    From the Saviour on the tree,
Pardon, peace, and cleansing bringing;
    Lost one, loved one, 't is for thee—
        Even thee.

2 Hear His love and mercy speaking,
    "Come and lay thy soul on me;
Though thy heart for sin be breaking,
    I have rest and peace for thee—
        Even thee."

The Sinner 101

Come then, now—to Jesus flying,
  From thy sin and woe be free;
Burdened, guilty, wounded, dying,
  Gladly will He welcome thee—
        Even thee.

Every sin shall be forgiven,
  Thou through grace a child shalt be—
Child of God, and heir of heaven,
  Yes, a mansion waits for thee—
        Even thee.

5 There in love for ever dwelling,
  Jesus all thy joy shall be,
And thy song shall still be telling
  All His mercy did for thee—
        Even thee.

EVEN ME
100.   8s and 7s.

1 LORD, I hear of showers of blessing
  Thou art scattering full and free;
Showers the thirsty land refreshing;
  Let some droppings fall on me,
        Even *me*.

2 Pass me not, oh! gracious Father,
  Sinful though my heart may be;
Thou might'st curse me—but the rather
  Let thy mercy light on me,
        Even *me*.

The Sinner.

3 Pass me not, oh! tender Saviour,
    Let me love and cling to thee;
I am longing for thy favor;
    When thou comest call for me,
        Even *me*.

4 Pass me not, oh! mighty Spirit,
    Thou canst make the blind to see;
Witnesser of Jesus' merit,
    Speak the word of power to me,
        Even *me*.

5 Love of God—so pure and changeless;
    Blood of God—so rich and free;
Grace of God—so strong and boundless;
    Magnify it all in me,
        Even *me*.

101.   11s.

1 DELAY not, delay not; O sinner! draw near;
    The waters of life are now flowing for thee:
No price is demanded; the Saviour is here;
    Redemption is purchased, salvation is free.

2 Delay not, delay not; why longer abuse
    The love and compassion of Jesus, thy God?
A fountain is opened, how canst thou refuse
    To wash and be cleansed in his par-

The Sinner.

Delay not, delay not; O sinner! to come,
  For mercy still lingers, and calls thee to-day;
Her voice is not heard in the shades of the tomb;
  Her message, unheeded, will soon pass away.

Delay not, delay not; the Spirit of grace,
  Long grieved and resisted may take his sad flight;
And leave thee in darkness to finish thy race,
  To sink in the gloom of eternity's night.

02.   P. M.*

Just as I am, without one plea,
But that thy blood was shed for me,
And that thou bid'st me come to Thee,
    O Lamb of God, I come!

Just as I am, and waiting not
To rid my soul of one dark blot,
To Thee, whose blood can cleanse each spot,
    O Lamb of God, I come!

---

*The metre of this most beautiful hymn is one with lich few are acquainted. It may, however, be sung a long measure tune, by repeating the words: "I me," in the fourth line of each verse.

The Sinner.

3 Just as I am, though tossed about
With many a conflict, many a doubt,
With fears within and wars without,
  O Lamb of God, I come!

4 Just as I am, poor, wretched, blind,
Sight, riches, healing of the mind,
Yea, all I need, in Thee to find,
  O Lamb of God, I come!

5 Just as I am—Thou wilt receive,
Wilt welcome, pardon, cleanse, relieve,
Because thy promise I believe—
  O Lamb of God, I come!

6 Just as I am—Thy love unknown
Has broken every barrier down;
Now to be Thine, yea, Thine alone—
  O Lamb of God, I come!

103.   P M.

1 JUST as thou art, without one trace
Of love, or joy, or inward grace,
Or meetness for the heavenly place,
  O guilty sinner! come.

2 Thy sins I bore on Calvary's tree;
The stripes thy due were laid on me,
That peace and pardon might be free—
  O wretched sinner! come.

The Sinner.

Come, leave thy burden at the cross;
Count all thy gains but empty dross:
My grace repays all earthly loss—
    O needy sinner! come.

Come, hither bring thy boding fears,
Thy aching heart, thy bursting tears;
'T is mercy's voice salutes thine ears;
    O trembling sinner! come.

"The Spirit and the bride say, Come;"
Rejoicing saints re-echo, Come;
Who faints, who thirsts, who will, may come:
    Thy Saviour bids thee come.

104.   S. M.

1 GRACE! 't is a charming sound,
    Harmonious to mine ear:
Heaven with the echo shall resound,
    And all the earth shall hear.

2 Grace first contrived the way
    To save rebellious man:
And all the steps *that* grace display,
    Which drew the wondrous plan.

3 Grace led my roving feet
    To tread the heavenly road;
And new supplies each hour I meet,
    While pressing on to God.

4 Grace all the work shall crown
   Through everlasting days;
It lays in heaven the topmost stone,
   And well deserves the praise.

105.   7s.

1 GRACIOUS Lord, incline thine ear,
My requests vouchsafe to hear:
Much distress'd with guilt am I;
Give me Jesus, or I die.

2 Lord, deny me what thou wilt,
Only take away my guilt:
Mourning at thy feet I lie;
Give me Jesus, or I die.

3 Thou dost freely save the lost,
In thy mercy I would trust:
With my earnest suit comply;
Give me Jesus, or I die.

4 O my God, what shall I say?
Take, O take my sins away:
Jesus' blood to me apply;
Give me Jesus, or I die.

106.   L. C. M.

1 WHEN thou my righteous judge, shalt come
  To take thy ransomed people home,
    Shall I among them stand?
Shall such a worthless worm as I,
Who sometimes am afraid to die,
    Be found at thy right hand?

I love to meet among them now,
Before thy gracious feet to bow,
  Though vilest of them all;
But can I bear the piercing thought,
What if my name should be left out,
  When thou for them shalt call?

Prevent, prevent it by thy grace:
Be thou, dear Lord, my hiding place
  In this the accepted day;
Thy pardoning voice, O let me hear,
To still my unbelieving fear,
  Nor let me fall, I pray.

Let me among thy saints be found,
Whene'er the archangel's trump shall
    sound,
  To see thy smiling face;
Then loudest of the crowd I'll sing,
While heaven's resounding mansions
    ring
  With shouts of sovereign grace.

107.   C. M.

1 COME, trembling sinner, in whose breast
    A thousand thoughts revolve;
Come, with your guilt and fear oppressed,
    And make this last resolve:

2 I'll go to Jesus, though my sin
    Hath like a mountain rose:
  I know his courts, I'll enter in,
    Whatever may oppose.

3 Perhaps he will admit my plea,
    Perhaps will hear my prayer;
  But if I perish I will pray,
    And perish only there.

4 I can but perish if I go;
    I am resolved to try;
  For if I stay away, I know
    I must for ever die.

108   C. M.

1 ALAS! and did my Saviour bleed?
    My great deliverer die?
  Would he devote that sacred head
    For such a worm as I?

2 Was it for crimes that I had done
    He groaned upon the tree?
  Amazing pity! grace unknown!
    And love beyond degree!

3 Well might the sun in darkness hide,
    And shut his glories in,
  When Christ, his mighty Maker, died
    For man the creature's sin.

Thus might I hide my blushing face
  While his dear cross appears;
Dissolve my heart in thankfulness,
  And melt mine eyes to tears.

But drops of grief can ne'er repay
  The debt of love I owe:
Here, Lord, I give myself away;
  'T is all that I can do.

09.   S. M.

Jesus! I come to thee,
  A sinner doomed to die;
My only refuge is thy cross—
  Here at thy feet I lie.

Can mercy reach my case,
  And all my sins remove?
Break, O my God! this heart of stone,
  And melt it by thy love.

Too long my soul has gone,
  Far from my God, astray;
I've sported on the brink of hell,
  In sin's delusive way.

But, Lord! my heart is fixed—
  I hope in thee alone;
Break off the chains of sin and death,
  And bind me to thy throne.

5 Thy blood can cleanse my heart,
   Thy hand can wipe my tears;
Oh! send thy blessed Spirit down
   To banish all my fears.

6 Then shall my soul arise,
   From sin and Satan free;
Redeemed from hell and every foe,
   I'll trust alone in thee.

110. 11s.

1 How firm a foundation, ye saints of t
      Lord,
   Is laid for your faith in his excelle
      word!
   What more can he say than to you
      hath said—
   You who unto Jesus for refuge have fle

2 Fear not, I am with thee, Oh! be
      dismayed,
   I—I am thy God, and will still give tl
      · aid;
   I'll strengthen thee, help thee, and ca
      thee to stand,
   Upheld by my righteous, omnipot
      hand.

3 When through the deep waters I cause thee to go,
The rivers of sorrow shall not thee o'erflow;
For I will be with thee, thy troubles to bless,
And sanctify to thee thy deepest distress.

4 When through fiery trials thy pathway shall lie,
My grace all-sufficient shall be thy supply;
The flame shall not hurt thee — I only design
Thy dross to consume and thy gold to refine.

5 E'en down to old age all my people shall prove
My sovereign, eternal, unchangeable love;
And, when hoary hairs shall their temples adorn,
Like lambs they shall still in my bosom be borne.

6 The soul that on Jesus hath leaned for repose
I will not, I cannot, desert to his foes;
That soul, though all hell should endeavor to shake,
I'll never—no, never—no, never forsake.

111. C. M.

1 Am I a soldier of the cross,
   A follower of the Lamb,
And shall I fear to own his cause,
   Or blush to speak his name?

2 Must I be carried to the skies
   On flowery beds of ease,
While others fought to win the prize
   And sailed through bloody seas?

3 Are there no foes for me to face?
   Must I not stem the flood?
Is this dark world a friend to grace,
   To help me on to God?

4 Sure I must fight, if I would reign;
   Increase my courage, Lord;
I'll bear the toil, endure the pain,
   Supported by thy word.

5 Thy saints in all this glorious war
   Shall conquer, though they die;
They see the triumph from afar,
   With faith's discerning eye.

6 When that illustrious day shall rise
   And all thine armies shine
In robes of victory through the skies
   The glory shall be thine.

112. C. M.

1 I'M not ashamed to own my Lord,
Nor to defend his cause;
Maintain the honor of his word,
The glory of his cross.

2 Jesus, my God, I know his name,
His name is all my trust;
Nor will he put my soul to shame,
Nor let my hope be lost.

3 Firm as his throne his promise stands,
And he can well secure
What I've committed to his hands
Till the decisive hour.

4 Then will he own my worthless name
Before his Father's face,
And in the new Jerusalem
Appoint my soul a place.

113. 5s, 6s, and 9s.

1 How happy are they
Who the Saviour obey,
And have laid up their treasures above!
Oh! what tongue can express
The sweet comfort and peace
Of a soul in its earliest love?

2 'T was heaven below
  My Redeemer to know,
And the angels could do nothing more
  Than to fall at his feet,
  And his story repeat,
And the Saviour of sinners adore.

3 Oh! the rapturous height
  Of that holy delight
Which I felt in his life-giving blood!
  Of my Saviour possessed,
  I was perfectly blest,
As if filled with the fulness of God.

4 Then, all the day long,
  Was my Jesus my song,
And redemption through faith in his na
  Oh! that all might believe,
  And salvation receive,
And their song and their joy be the s

114.   L. M.

1 STAND up, my soul, shake off thy f
    And gird the gospel armor on;
  March to the gates of endless joy,
    Where Jesus, thy great captain's

2 Hell and thy sins resist thy course,
    But hell and sin are vanquished
  Thy Jesus nailed them to the cross,
    And sung the triumph when He

3 What though thy inward lusts rebel?
    'T is but a struggling gasp for life:
  The 'weapons of victorious grace
    Shall slay thy sins and end the strife.

4 Then let my soul march boldly on,
    Press forward to the heavenly gate;
  There peace and joy eternal reign,
    And glittering robes for conquerors wait.

5 There shall I wear a starry crown,
    And triumph in almighty grace;
  While all the armies of the skies
    Join in my glorious leader's praise.

115.   7s and 6s.

1 BENEATH the cross of Jesus
    I lay me down to feast
  On him, my bleeding sacrifice,
    My altar, and my priest.

2 Beneath the cross of Jesus
    I lay me down to feel
  His peace and joy most precious,
    My griefs and sorrows heal.

3 Beneath the cross of Jesus
    I lay me down to sing
  "The grave has lost its victory,
    And death its venomed sting."

4 Beneath the cross of Jesus
   I lay me down to die,
 Till borne by blessed angels
   To his bright home on high.

5 Beneath the cross of Jesus
   I'll wonder and adore,
 And sing his endless praises
   With saints for evermore.

6 A harp I'll get from Jesus,
   And tune it loud and long;
 The cross and blood of Jesus
   My everlasting song.

116. L. M.

1 Awake, our souls! away our fears,
   Let every trembling thought be gone:
 Awake, and run the heavenly race,
   And put a cheerful courage on.

2 True, 't is a straight and thorny road,
   And mortal spirits tire and faint;
 But they forget the mighty God
   Who feeds the strength of ev'ry saint

3 The mighty God, whose matchless power
   Is ever new, and ever young;
 And firm endures, while endless years
   Their everlasting circles run.

4 From thee, the overflowing spring,
 Our souls shall drink a full supply;
While such as trust their native strength
 Shall melt away, and droop, and die.

5 Swift as an eagle cuts the air
 We'll mount aloft to thine abode;
On wings of love our souls shall fly,
 Nor tire upon the heavenly road.

117.   7s.

1 SLEEP not, soldier of the cross!
 Foes are lurking all around;
Think not here to find repose:
 This is but thy battle-ground.

2 Up! and take thy shield and sword;
 Up! it is the call of heaven:
Shrink not faithless from thy Lord;
 Nobly strive as he hath striven.

3 Break through all the force of ill;
 Tread the might of passion down—
Struggling onward, onward still,
 To the conqu'ring Saviour's crown!

4 Through the midst of toil and pain,
 Let this thought ne'er leave thy breast:
Every triumph thou dost gain
 Makes more sweet thy coming rest.

118. 10s and 11s.

1 Begone, unbelief! my Saviour is near,
And for my relief will surely appear:
By prayer let me wrestle, and he will perform;
With Christ in the vessel, I smile at the storm.

2 Though dark be my way, since Christ is my guide,
'T is *mine* to obey, 't is His to provide:
Though cisterns be broken, and creatures all fail,
The word he has spoken shall surely prevail.

3 His love, in time past, forbids me to think
He'll leave me at last in trouble to sink;
Each sweet Ebenezer I have in review
Confirms his good pleasure to help me quite through.

4 Why should I complain of want or distress,
Temptation or pain? he told me no less;
The heirs of salvation, I know from his word,
Through much tribulation must follow their Lord.

5 Since all that I meet shall work for my good,
The bitter is sweet, the medicine is food:
Though painful at present, 't will cease before long,
And then, O how pleasant the conqueror's song!

119. H. M.

1 By whom was David taught
    To aim the dreadful blow,
When he Goliath fought,
    And laid the Gittite low?
No sword nor spear the stripling took,
But chose a pebble from the brook.

2 'T was Israel's God and King
    Who sent him to the fight;
Who gave him strength to sling,
    And skill to aim aright?
Ye feeble saints, your strength endures,
Because young David's God is yours.

3 Who order'd Gideon forth
    To storm the invader's camp—
With arms of little worth,
    A pitcher, and a lamp?
The trumpets made his coming known;
And all the host was overthrown.

4 Oh! I have seen the day
    When with a single word—
God helping me to say,
    "My trust is in the Lord"—
My soul has quell'd a thousand foes,
Fearless of all that could oppose.

5 But unbelief, self-will,
    Self-righteousness, and pride—
How often do they steal
    My weapons from my side!
Yet David's Lord and Gideon's Friend
Will help his servants to the end.

120. C. M.

Didst thou, dear Jesus, suffer shame
    And bear the cross for me?
And shall I fear to own thy name,
    Or thy disciple be?

2 Inspire my soul with life divine,
    And make me truly bold;
Let knowledge, faith, and meekness shi
    Nor love nor zeal grow cold.

3 Let mockers scoff, the world defame,
    And treat me with disdain;
Still may I glory in thy name,
    And count reproach my gain.

4 To thee I cheerfully submit,
 And all my powers resign;
 Let wisdom point out what is fit,
 And I'll no more repine.

21.   8s and 7s.

My comrades all, on you I call,
 Arise and look around you:
How many foes, bound to oppose,
 Are waiting to confound you.
The trumpet calls from Zion's walls,
 Shake off your sleep and slumber:
Arise and pray, we'll win the day,
 Though we are few in number.

2 Now valiant prove for him you love,
 Confide in his great power:
Resolve to die, but never fly,
 His rock shall be your tower.
Our triumph 's sure, if we 'll endure,
 And urge the contest stronger:
The prize of life shall crown the strife,
 A few more struggles longer.

3 The conflict sore will soon be o'er,
 The trump of triumph sounded:
Our armor bright shall with delight
 At Jesus' feet be grounded.
Then God shall give, and we receive,
 The crowns of fadeless glory;
And long we 'll dwell in heaven to tell
 Love's all-immortal story.

122. 7s.—6-line.

1 When this passing world is done,
When has sunk yon glaring sun,
When we stand with Christ in glory
Looking o'er life's finished story,
Then, Lord, shall I fully know—
Not till then—how much I owe.

2 When I hear the wicked call
On the rocks and hills to fall;
When I see them start and shrink
On the fiery deluge brink,
Then, Lord, shall I fully know—
Not till then—how much I owe.

3 When I stand before the throne,
Dressed in beauty not my own,
When I see Thee as thou art,
Love thee with unsinning heart,
Then, Lord, shall I fully know—
Not till then—how much I owe.

4 Chosen not for good in me,
Wakened up from wrath to flee,
Hidden in the Saviour's side,
By the Spirit sanctified;
Teach me Lord, on earth to show,
By my love, how much I owe.

The Christian. 123

5 Oft I walk beneath the cloud,
Dark as midnight's gloomy shroud;
But when fear is at the height,
Jesus comes and all is light;
Blessed Jesus! bid me show
Doubting saints how much I owe.

23. S. M.

Give to the winds thy fears;
  Hope on, be not dismayed:
God hears thy sighs and counts thy tears;
  God shall lift up thy head.

Through waves, and clouds, and storms
  He gently clears thy way;
Wait thou his time: the darkest night
  Shall end in brightest day.

Far, far above thy thought
  His counsel shall appear,
When fully he the work hath wrought
  That caused thy needless fear.

What though thou rulest not!
  Yet heaven, and earth, and hell
Proclaim—God sitteth on the throne,
  And ruleth all things well.

124. 8s and 7s.—*6-line.*

1 GOD imposes not a burden
    Heavier than man can bear:
Nobly borne, it proves a guerdon
    Mortal man might hardly spare;
Tear the burden from his heart,
Man and all he loves would part.

2 Fear thou not, encounter boldly
    That which meets thee on thy way;
He who went before hath told thee
    Thou shalt overcome one day;
Nerve thy heart with strong assurance,
Brace thy limbs to long endurance.

3 Soldiers, face the hottest battle
    Till the day is bravely won,
Disregard the cannon's rattle,
    And the carnage and the gun;
Victory, achieved to-day,
Helps to-morrow on its way.

4 Shrink thou not, nor be faint-hearted
    In untoward circumstance—
Fires are quenched and waters parted
    For the saint's deliverance;
Fear thou not, what may befall thee,
Boldly go where duties call thee.

The Christian.

5 Patient striving, meek forbearing,
  Prayer, and faithful diligence—
Love, and sacrifice unsparing,
  Fail not of their recompense;
Water, dropping day by day,
Wears the hardest stone away.

25.   C. M.

In all my Lord's appointed ways
  My journey I 'll pursue;
"Hinder me not," ye much-loved saints,
  For I must go with you.

Through floods and flames, if Jesus lead,
  I 'll follow where he goes;
"Hinder me not," shall be my cry,
  Though earth and hell oppose.

Through duty, and through trials, too,
  I 'll go at his command:
"Hinder me not," for I am bound
  To my Immanuel's land.

And when my Saviour calls me home
  My joyful cry shall be,
"Hinder me not;" come, welcome death;
  I 'll gladly go with thee.

126. C. M.

1 How sweet, how heavenly is the sight,
When those who love the Lord
In one another's peace delight,
And so fulfil his word;

2 When each can feel his brother's sigh,
And with him bear a part;
When sorrows flow from eye to eye,
And joy from heart to heart;

3 When, free from envy, scorn, and pride
Our wishes all above,
Each can his brother's failings hide,
And show a brother's love.

4 Let love, in one delightful stream,
Through every bosom flow;
And union sweet, and dear esteem,
In every action glow.

5 Love is the golden chain that binds
The happy souls above;
And he's an heir of heaven who find
His bosom glow with love.

127. 8s.

1 The Christian warrior—see him stand
In the whole armor of his God:
The Spirit's sword is in his hand,
His feet are with the gospel shod

The Christian.

2 In panoply of truth complete,
　Salvation's helmet on his head:
With righteousness. a breastplate meet;
　And faith's broad shield before him spread,
3 Undaunted to the field he goes;
　Yet vain were skill and valor there,
Unless, to foil his legion-foes,
　The trustiest. weapon were "all-prayer."
4 With this omnipotence he moves,
　From this the alien armies flee,
Till more than conqueror he proves,
　Through Christ who gives him victory.
5 Thus, strong in his Redeemer's strength,
　Sin, death, and hell he tramples down,
Fights the good fight, and wins at length,
　Through mercy, an immortal crown.

128. 7s and 6s.

1 O FAINT and feeble-hearted,
　　Why thus cast down with fear?
Fresh aid shall be imparted;
　　Thy God unseen is near.
2 His eye can never slumber,
　　He marks thy cruel foes;
Observes their strength, their number,
　　And all thy weakness knows.

3 Though heavy clouds of sorrow
   Make dark thy path to-day,
 There may shine forth to-morrow
   Once more a cheering way.

4 Though doubts and griefs assailing
   Conceal heaven's fair abode;
 Yet now faith's power prevailing
   Should stay thy mind on God.

129. 7s.

1 Oft in sorrow, oft in woe,
Onward, Christian, onward go!
Fight the fight, maintain the strife,
Strengthened with the bread of life.

2 Onward, Christian, onward go!
Join the war and face the foe:
Will you flee in danger's hour?
Know you not your Captain's power?

3 Let your drooping heart be glad:
March, in heavenly armor clad;
Fight! nor think the battle long;
Soon shall victory tune your song.

4 Let not sorrow dim your eye;
Soon shall every tear be dry:
Let not fears your course impede;
Great your strength if great your need.

5 Onward, then, to battle move!
More than conqu'ror you shall prove;
Though opposed by many a foe,
Christian soldier, onward go!

130. L. M.

'T is by the faith of joys to come
  We walk through deserts dark as night,
Till we arrive at heaven, our home,
  Faith is our guide, and faith our light.

2 The want of sight she well supplies;
  She makes the pearly gates appear;
Far into distant worlds she pries,
  And brings eternal glories near.

3 Cheerful we tread the desert through,
  While faith inspires a heavenly ray,
Though lions roar and tempests blow,
  And rocks and dangers fill the way.

4 So Abram, by divine command,
  Left his own house to walk with God;
His faith beheld the promised land,
  And fired his zeal along the road.

131. S. M.

1 My soul, be on thy guard,
  Ten thousand foes arise;
And hosts of sin are pressing hard
  To draw thee from the skies.

2 O watch, and fight, and pray,
  The battle ne'er give o'er;
Renew it boldly every day,
  And help divine implore.

3 Ne'er think the victory won,
  Nor once at ease sit down;
Thy arduous work will not be done,
  Till thou hast got thy crown.

132.   *Tune—"Scots wha ha'e."*

1 SOLDIERS of the cross, arise!
Lo, your Captain from the skies,
Holding forth the glittering prize,
  Calls to victory!
Fear not, though the battle lower,
Firmly stand the trying hour,
Stand the tempter's utmost power,
  Spurn his slavery.

2 Who the cause of Christ would yield
Who would leave the battle-field?
Who would cast away his shield?
  Let him basely go:
Who for Zion's King will stand?
Who will join the faithful band?
Let him come with heart and hand,
  Let him face the foe.

Sorrow and Sickness. 131

3 By the mercies of our God,
By Immanuel's streaming blood
When alone for us he stood,
  Ne'er give up the strife:
Even to the latest breath
Hark to what your Captain saith:
Be thou faithful unto death,
  Take the crown of life.

133.   C. M.
1 FATHER, whate'er of earthly bliss
    Thy sovereign will denies,
  Accepted at thy throne of grace,
    Let this petition rise:

2 "Give me a calm, a thankful heart,
    From every murmur free;
  The blessings of thy grace impart,
    And make me live to thee.

3 "Let the sweet hope that I am thine,
    My life and death attend;
  Thy presence through my journey shine,
    And crown my journey's end."

134.   6s.
1 MY Jesus, as Thou wilt!
    Oh, may Thy will be mine!
  Into Thy hand of love
    I would my all resign.

Through sorrow or through joy,
  Conduct me as Thine own,
And help me still to say,
  "My Lord, Thy will be done!"

2 My Jesus, as Thou wilt!
  If needy here, and poor,
Give me thy people's bread,
  Their portion rich and sure.
The manna of thy word
  Let my soul feed upon;
And if all else should fail—
  "My Lord, Thy will be done!"

3 My Jesus, as Thou wilt!
  If loved ones must depart,
Suffer not sorrow's flood
  To overwhelm my heart:
For they are blest with Thee,
  Their race and conflict won:
Let me but follow them:
  "My Lord, Thy will be done!"

4 My Jesus, as Thou wilt!
  When death itself draws nigh,
To thy dear wounded side
  I would for refuge fly.
Leaning on thee, to go
  Where Thou before hast gone;
The rest as Thou shalt please:
  "My Lord, Thy will be done!"

Sorrow and Sickness.

5 My Jesus, as Thou wilt!
All shall be well for me:
Each changing future scene
I gladly trust with Thee.
Straight to my home above
I travel calmly on,
And sing, in life or death,
"My Lord, Thy will be done!"

135.   P. M.

1 My God, my Father, while I stray
Far from my home, on life's rough way,
Oh! teach me from my heart to say,
  " Thy will be done."

2 If Thou should'st call me to resign
What most I prize—it ne'er was mine;
I only yield thee what was Thine;
  " Thy will be done."

3 E'en if again I ne'er should see
The friend more dear than life to me,
Ere long we both shall be with Thee;
  " Thy will be done."

4 Should pining sickness waste away
My life in premature decay,
My Father, still I strive to say,
  " Thy will be done."

5 If but my fainting heart be blest
With thy sweet Spirit for its guest,
My God, to thee I leave the rest,
  "Thy will be done."

6 Renew my will from day to day,
Blend it with Thine, and take away
All that now makes it hard to say,
  "Thy will be done."

7 Then when on earth I breathe no more
The prayer oft mixed with tears before,
I'll sing upon a happier shore,
  "Thy will be done."

136.   7s.

1 Jesus. Saviour, sympathize
With thy servant's agonies;
In thy lifetime thou hast known
Racking pains that made thee moan—
Pain of body, grief of mind,
Shame and suffering combined.

2 With thy sanctifying hand
Touch me gently, and command
Some soft drops of dewy balm
To be shed with potent charm;
Comfort was to thee imparted—
Comfort thou the broken-hearted.

Sorrow and Sickness.

3 Not alone the token thou
  Of an angry Father's brow;
  Rather of his willingness
  To renew, receive, and bless;
  Welcome then be thou to me,
  Even through sharpest agony.

4 Only, in each torturing hour,
  Let me feel, O God of power,
  That thy gentle hand alone
  Gives the pain that makes me moan;
  That, by grace, I may attain
  Fortitude in suffering pain.

137.   C. M.

1 AFFLICTION is a stormy deep,
    Where wave responds to wave;
  Though o'er my head the billows roll,
    I know the Lord can save.

2 The hand that now withholds my joys
    Can yet restore my peace;
  And he who bade the tempest roar
    Can bid the tempest cease.

3 In darkest watches of the night
    I'll count his mercies o'er,
  I'll praise him for ten thousand past,
    And humbly sue for more.

4 When darkness and when sorrow rose,
    And pressed on every side,
The Lord has still sustained my steps,
    And still has been my guide.

5 Here will I rest and build my hope,
    Nor murmur at his rod;
He's more than all the world to me—
    My Saviour and my God.

138.   C. M.

1 My God, the spring of all my joys,
    The life of my delights,
The glory of my brightest days,
    And comfort of my nights;

2 In darkest shades if he appear,
    My dawning is begun;
He is my soul's bright morning star,
    And He my rising sun.

3 The opening heavens around me shine
    With beams of sacred bliss,
While Jesus shows his heart is mine,
    And whispers I am His.

4 My soul would leave this heavy clay
    At that transporting word;
Run up with joy the shining way,
    To embrace my dearest Lord.

Sorrow and Sickness. 137

Fearless of hell and ghastly death,
  I 'd break through every foe;
The wings of love and arms of faith
  Should bear me conqueror through.

2. 7s.

Faint not, Christian! though the road
Leading to thy blest abode
Darksome be, and dangerous too,
Christ, thy guide, will bring thee through.

Faint not, Christian! though in rage
Satan would thy soul engage;
Gird on faith's anointed shield,
Bear it to the battle-field.

Faint not, Christian! though the world
Has its hostile flag unfurled;
Hold the cross of Jesus fast,
Thou shalt overcome at last.

Faint not, Christian! though within
There 's a heart so prone to sin;
Christ the Lord is over all,
He 'll not suffer thee to fall.

Faint not, Christian! though thy God
Smite thee with his chastening rod;
Smite he must, with father's care,
That he may his love declare.

6 Faint not, Christian! look on high
See the harpers in the sky;
Patient wait, and thou wilt join—
Chant with them of love divine.

140. C. M.

1 Jesus, my sorrow lies too deep
For human ministry;
It knows not how to tell itself
To any but to Thee.

2 Thou dost remember still amid
The glories of God's throne,
The sorrows of mortality,
For they were once Thine own.

3 Thy risen life but fits Thee more
For kindly sympathy;
Thy love, unhindered, rests upon
Each bruised branch in Thee.

4 Jesus! my fainting spirit brings
Its fearfulness to Thee;
Thine eye, at least, can penetrate
The clouded mystery.

5 It is enough, my precious Lord,
Thy tender sympathy!
My every sin and sorrow can
Repose itself on Thee.

C. M.

When languor and disease invade
  This trembling house of clay,
'T is sweet to look beyond my pains,
  And long to fly away.

Sweet to look inward, and attend
  The whispers of his love;
Sweet to look upward to the place
  Where Jesus pleads above.

Sweet to reflect how grace divine
  My sins on Jesus laid;
Sweet to remember that his blood
  My debt of suffering paid.

Sweet on his faithfulness to rest,
  Whose love can never end;
Sweet on his covenant of grace
  For all things to depend.

Sweet, in the confidence of faith,
  To trust his firm decrees;
Sweet to lie passive in his hand,
  And know no will but his.

2. S. M.

1 Kindly the Lord appeared
  In nature's trying hour;
His love my sinking spirit cheered;
  I felt his strengthening power.

Sorrow and Sickness.

2 He found me on the bed
    Of languishing and pain;
And bade me lean on him my head,
    Nor seek his aid in vain.

3 I saw his mighty arm
    Stretched o'er the rolling wave;
He snatched my life from threatening
    harm,
And showed his power to save.

4 How, then, can I refuse
    The glad and grateful strain?
The Lord my wasteful strength renews,
    And makes me well again.

5 Oh! may my future days
    My gratitude display;
Nor *speak* alone, but *live* thy praise,
    Through each revolving day.

143.   C. M.

1 My God! thy service well demands
    The remnant of my days;
Why was this fleeting breath renewed
    But to renew thy praise?

2 Thine arms of everlasting love
    Did this weak frame sustain,
When life was hovering o'er the grave
    And nature sunk with pain.

Calmly I bowed my fainting head,
  On thy dear, faithful breast;
Pleased to obey my Father's call
  To his eternal rest.

Into thy hands, my Saviour God!
  Did I my soul resign,
In firm reliance on that truth,
  Which made salvation mine.

Back from the borders of the grave
  At thy command I come;
Nor will I ask a speedier flight
  To my celestial home.

Where thou appointest mine abode,
  There would I choose to be;
For in thy presence death is life,
  And earth is heaven with thee.

4.   P. M.

1 Saviour, thy love alone can fill
  And satisfy the human heart;
  Can turn to good each seeming ill,
      And peace impart.

2. Then deign to make thyself to me,
  While here a sojourner I roam,
  A living, bright reality,
      My rest, my home.

3 More present to faith's inward sight
Than earthly objects to my eye,
My hourly well-spring of delight,
    Which ne'er runs dry.

4 If of some cherished good bereft,
Too fondly prized, hard to resign,
Still let me feel enough is left,
    If thou art mine.

5 In sorrow, be thy love my balm—
A balm omnipotent to heal;
In joy, to sanctify and calm—
    That love reveal.

6 More intimately be thou nigh
Then e'en the dearest earthly frien[d]
Bound by that strong, mysterious t[ie]
    Death cannot rend.

7 Let all around me clearly trace
A growing likeness, Lord, to thee;
A trophy of transforming grace
    Oh, let me be!

145.   C. L. M.

1 When I can trust my all with (God)
  In trial's fearful hour;
Bow all resigned beneath his ro[d]
  And bless his saving power;
A joy springs up amid distress,
A fountain in the wilderness.

Sorrow and Sickness. 143

Oh! to be brought to Jesus' feet,
  Though trials fix me there,
's still a privilege most sweet,
  For he will hear my prayer;
Though sighs and tears its language be,
The Lord is nigh to answer me.

Then, blessed be the hand that gave,
  Still blessed when it takes;
Blessed be he who smites to save,
  Who heals the heart he breaks:
Perfect and true are all his ways
Whom heaven adores and death obeys.

6.   8s, 7s, and 4s.
O my soul, what means this sadness,
  Wherefore art thou thus cast down?
Let thy griefs be turned to gladness;
  Bid thy restless fears begone:
    Look to Jesus,
  And rejoice in his dear name.

What though Satan's strong temptations
  Vex and grieve thee day by day,
And thy sinful inclinations
  Often fill thee with dismay?
    Thou shalt conquer
  Through the Lamb's redeeming blood.

3 Though ten thousand ills beset thee
   From without and from within,
Jesus saith he 'll ne'er forget thee,
   But will save from hell and sin:
     He is faithful
   To perform his gracious word.

147.   L. M.

1 WHEN struggling on the bed of pain,
And earth and all its joys are vain,
How sweet, my God, to know thy po[wer]
Sustains me in the trying hour.

2 How rich and precious sounds that l[ove]
That tells of rest and joys above,
And lulls my troubled heart to rest
Upon my blessed Saviour's breast.

3 There, still, while life's warm curr[ents]
   rush,
My soul would all her sorrows hush,
Nor ever yield to dark despair,
For light, and life, and peace are th[ere].

4 Helper and Hope thou ever art,
To heal the wounded, broken heart;
Oh! let me hear thy pardoning voic[e]
And bid my broken bones rejoice.

Sorrow and Sickness.

Then shall my cheerful, grateful tongue
In rapturous strains thy praise prolong;
My ransomed soul adore thy grace,
And swifter run the heavenly race.

18.   7s.

1 Go to dark Gethsemane,
   Ye who feel the tempter's power;
Your Redeemer's conflict see;
   Watch with him one bitter hour;
Turn not from his griefs away;
Learn of Jesus Christ to pray.

2 Follow to the judgment hall,
   View the Lord of life arraigned;
O the wormwood and the gall!
   O the pangs his soul sustained!
Shun not suffering, shame, or loss;
Learn of him to bear the cross.

3 Calvary's mournful mountain climb;
   There, adoring at his feet,
Mark that miracle of time,
   God's own sacrifice complete;
"It is finished," hear him cry;
Learn of Jesus Christ to die.

Dying and Death.

4 Early hasten to the tomb
  Where they laid his breathless clay:
All is solitude and gloom;
  Who hath taken him away?
Christ has risen, he seeks the skies;
Saviour, teach us so to rise.

149.   8s, 7s, and 4s.

1 GUIDE me, O thou great Jehovah,
    Pilgrim through this barren land;
  I am weak, but thou art mighty,
    Hold me with thy powerful hand:
      Bread of heaven
    Feed me till I want no more.

2 Open now the crystal fountain
    Whence the healing streams do flow;
  Let the fiery, cloudy pillar
    Lead me all my journey through;
      Strong Deliverer,
    Be thou still my strength and shield.

3 When I tread the verge of Jordan,
    Bid my anxious fears subside:
  Death of death, and hell's destruction,
    Land me safe on Canaan's side;
      Songs of praises
    I will ever give to thee.

150.   8s and 7s.

1 GENTLY, Lord! O gently lead us
   Through this lonely vale of tears—
Through the changes thou 'st decreed us,
   Till our last great change appears:
O refresh us with thy blessing,
   O sustain us with thy grace!
May thy mercies, never ceasing,
   Fit us for thy dwelling place.

2 When temptation's darts assail us,
   When in devious paths we stray,
Let thy goodness never fail us—
   Lead us in thy perfect way:
In the hour of pain and anguish,
   In the hour when death draws near,
Suffer not our hearts to languish,
   Suffer not our souls to fear.

3 When this mortal life is ended,
   Bid us in thine arms to rest,
Till by angel bands attended,
   We awake among the blest:
O refresh us with thy blessing—
   O sustain us with thy grace!
May thy mercies, never ceasing,
   Fit us for thy dwelling place.

151. C. M.

1 WHEN waves of sorrow round me swell,
  My soul is not dismayed;
 I hear a voice I know full well,
 " 'T is I, be not afraid."

2 When black the threat'ning clouds appear,
  And storms my path invade,
 That voice shall tranquillize each fear,
 " 'T is I, be not afraid."

3 There is a gulf that must be crossed—
  Saviour! be near to aid;
 Whisper, when my frail bark is tossed,
 " 'T is I, be not afraid."

4 There is a dark and fearful vale,
  Death hides within its shade;
 Oh! say, when flesh and heart shall fail,
 " 'T is I, be not afraid."

152. 8s and 7s.

1 My days are gliding swiftly by,
  And I, a pilgrim stranger,
 Would not detain them as they fly—
  Those hours of toil and danger.

Dying and Death.

We'll gird our loins, my brethren dear,
  Our heavenly home discerning;
Our absent Lord has left us word
  Let every lamp be burning.

Should coming days be cold and dark,
  We need not cease our singing;
That perfect rest naught can molest,
  Where golden harps are ringing.

Let sorrow's rudest tempest blow,
  Each chord on earth to sever;
Our King says come, and there's our home,
  For ever, oh! for ever!

Chorus.

For oh! we stand on Jordan's strand,
  Our friends are passing over,
And, just before, the shining shore
  We may almost discover.

53.   P. M.

1 ONE sweetly solemn thought
    Comes to me o'er and o'er;
I'm nearer my home to-day
    Than I've ever been before.

2 Nearer my Father's house,
    Where the many mansions be;
Nearer the great white throne,
    Nearer the jasper sea:

3 Nearer the bound of life,
    Where we lay our burdens down:
  Nearer leaving my cross,
    Nearer wearing my crown.

4 But lying darkly between,
    Winding down through the night,
  Is that dim and unknown stream
    Which leads at last to light.

5 Father! perfect my trust,
    Strengthen my feeble faith:
  Let me feel as if I trod
    The shore of the river Death.

6 For even now my feet
    May stand upon its brink—
  I may be nearer my home,
    Nearer now than I think.

154.   C. M.

1 O FOR an overcoming faith,
    To cheer my dying hours;
  To triumph o'er the monster death,
    And all his frightful powers!

2 Joyful, with all the strength I have,
    My quiv'ring lips should sing:
  "Where is thy boasted vict'ry, grave?
    And where the monster's sting?"

Dying and Death.

3 If sin be pardon'd, I 'm secure ;
  Death has no sting beside :
The law gives sin its damning power,
  But Christ, my ransom, died.

4 Now to the God of victory
  Immortal thanks be paid ;
Who makes us conqu'rors, while we die,
  Through Christ our living head.

155. C. M.

1 O THOU, from whom all goodness flows,
  I lift my soul to thee ;
In all my sorrows, conflicts, woes,
  O Lord, remember me !

2 When on my aching, burdened heart
  My sins lie heavily,
Thy pardon grant, new peace impart ;
  Then, Lord, remember me ;

3 When trials sore obstruct my way,
  And ills I cannot flee,
Oh, let my strength be as my day—
  Dear Lord, remember me !

4 When in the solemn hour of death
  I wait thy just decree ;
Be this the prayer of my last breath :
  Now, Lord, remember me !

5 And when before thy throne I stand,
  And lift my soul to thee,
Then, with thy saints at thy right hand,
  O Lord, remember me!

156. 7s.

1 WHEN along life's thorny road
Faints the soul beneath the load,
By its cares and sins opprest,
Finds on earth no peace or rest:
When the wily tempter 's near,
Filling us with doubts and fear,
Jesus, to thy feet we flee,
Jesus, we will look to Thee.

2 Thou, our Saviour, from the throne,
List'nest to thy people's moan;
Thou, the living Head, dost share
Every pang thy members bear.
Full of tenderness thou art;
Thou wilt heal the broken heart;
Full of power, Thine arm shall quell
All the rage and might of hell!

3 By Thy tears o'er Lazarus shed,
By Thy power to raise the dead,
By Thy meekness under scorn,
By Thy stripes and crown of thorn.

Dying and Death. 153

By that rich and precious blood,
That hath made our peace with God,
Jesus, to thy feet we flee;
Jesus, we will cling to Thee.

4 Mighty to redeem and save,
Thou hast overcome the grave;
Thou the bars of death hast riven,
Opened wide the gates of heaven;
Soon in glory thou shalt come,
Taking thy poor pilgrims home;
Jesus, then we all shall be,
Ever — ever — Lord, with Thee.

157. C. M.

1 .O FOR a faith that will not shrink
    Though pressed by many a foe;
That will not tremble on the brink
    Of poverty or woe.

2 That will not murmur nor complain
    Beneath the chastening rod;
But in the hour of grief or pain
    Can lean upon its God.

3 A faith that keeps the narrow way,
    By truth restrained and led,
And with a pure and heavenly ray
    Lights up a dying bed.

4 Lord, give me such a faith as this,
  And then, whate'er may come,
I'll taste e'en here the hallowed bliss
  Of an eternal home.

158.   L. M.

1 Why should we start and fear to die,
  What timorous worms we mortals!
Death is the gate of endless joy,
  And yet we dread to enter there.

2 The pains, the groans. and dying strife,
  Fright our approaching souls away;
Still we shrink back again to life,
  Fond of our prison and our clay.

3 Oh! if my Lord would come and meet,
  My soul would stretch her wings in haste,
Fly fearless through death's iron gate,
  Nor feel the terrors as she passed.

4 Jesus can make a dying bed
  Feel soft as downy pillows are,
While on his breast I lean my head,
  And breathe my life out sweetly there.

159.   S. M.

1 Oh! for the death of those
  Who slumber in the Lord!
Oh! be like theirs my last repose,
  Like theirs my last reward!

Their bodies in the ground
  In silent hope may lie,
Till the last trumpet's joyful sound
  Shall call them to the sky.

Their ransomed spirits soar,
  On wings of faith and love,
To meet the Saviour they adore,
  And reign with him above.

With us their names shall live
  Through long succeeding years,
Embalmed with all our hearts can give,
  Our praises and our tears.

Oh! for the death of those
  Who slumber in the Lord!
Oh! be like theirs my last repose,
  Like theirs my last reward!

S. M.

Prepare me, gracious God,
  To stand before thy face;
Thy spirit must the work perform,
  For it is all of grace.

In Christ's obedience clothe,
  And wash me in his blood:
So shall I lift my head with joy,
  Among the sons of God.

Dying and Death.

3 Do thou my sins subdue,
   Thy sovereign love make known;
The spirit of my mind renew,
   And save me in thy Son.

4 Let me attest thy power,
   Let me thy goodness prove,
Till my full soul can hold no more
   Of everlasting love.

161. C. M.

1 Why do we mourn departing friends,
   Or shake at death's alarms?
'T is but the voice that Jesus sends,
   To call them to his arms.

2 Are we not tending upward, too,
   As fast as time can move?
Nor should we wish our hours more slow
   To keep us from our love.

3 Why should we tremble to convey
   Their bodies to the tomb?
There the dear flesh of Jesus lay,
   And left a long perfume.

4 The graves of all the saints He blest,
   And softened every bed;
Where should the dying members rest,
   But with their dying Head?

Dying and Death. 157

5 Thence He arose, ascending high,
   And showed our feet the way;
Up to the Lord our flesh shall fly,
   At the great rising day.

62.   L. M.

Asleep in Jesus! blessed sleep!
From which none ever wake to weep;
A calm and undisturbed repose,
Unbroken by the last of foes.

Asleep in Jesus! oh, how sweet
To be for such a slumber meet!
With holy confidence to sing
That death hath lost its venomed sting!

Asleep in Jesus! peaceful rest!
Whose waking is supremely blest;
No fear, no woe, shall dim that hour
Which manifests the Saviour's power.

Asleep in Jesus! far from thee
Thy kindred and their graves may be;
But thine is still a blessed sleep,
From which none ever wakes to weep.

Asleep in Jesus! oh, for me
May such a blissful refuge be!
Securely shall my ashes lie,
And wait the summons from on high.

Dying and Death.

163. 11s.

1 I WOULD not live alway! I ask not to sta[y]
Where storm after storm rises dark o'e[r]
the way;
The few lurid mornings that dawn on [us]
here
Are enough for life's woes, full enough f[or]
its cheer.

2 I would not live alway, thus fettered b[y]
sin;
Temptation without and corruption with
in:
E'en the rapture of pardon is mingle[d]
with fears,
And the cup of thanksgiving with [peni]
tent tears.

3 I would not live alway; no—welcome th[e]
tomb;
Since Jesus has lain there, I dread no[t]
its gloom:
There, sweet be my rest, till He bid m[e]
arise,
To hail Him in triumph descending th[e]
skies.

4 Who, who would live alway, away fro[m]
his God;

way from yon heaven, that blissful abode,
here the rivers of pleasure flow o'er the bright plains,
nd the noontide of glory eternally reigns:
'here the saints of all ages in harmony meet,
heir Saviour and brethren, transported to greet;
'hile the anthems of rapture unceasingly roll,
nd the smile of the Lord is the feast of the soul?

C. M.

HEN rising from the bed of death,
  O'erwhelmed with guilt and fear,
see my Maker, face to face,
  O how shall I appear?

yet, while pardon may be found,
  And mercy may be sought,
Iy heart with inward horror shrinks,
  And trembles at the thought,

When thou, O Lord, shalt stand disclosed
  In majesty severe,
And sit in judgment on my soul,
  O how shall I appear?

4 But thou hast told the troubled mind
    Who does her sins lament,
That faith in Christ's atoning blood
    Shall endless woe prevent.

5 Then never shall my soul despair
    Her pardon to procure,
Who knows thine only Son has died
    To make that pardon sure.

165.   L. M.—6-*line.*

1 My God! I know that I must die—
    My mortal life is passing hence;
On earth I neither hope nor try
    To find a lasting residence.
Then teach me by Thy heavenly grace
With joy and peace my death to face.

2 My God! I know not *when* I die,
    What is the moment or the hour—
How soon the clay may broken lie,
    How quickly pass away the flower.
Then may thy child prepared be
Through time to meet eternity.

3 My God! I know not *how* I die,
    For death has many ways to come—
In dark, mysterious agony,
    Or gently as a sleep to some.
Just as thou wilt! if but it be
For ever blessed, Lord, with Thee.

My God! I know not *where* I die,
  Where is my grave, beneath what
    strand,
Yet from its gloom I do rely
  To be delivered by Thy hand.
Content, I take what spot is mine,
Since all the earth, my Lord, is Thine.

My gracious God! when I must die,
  Oh! bear my happy soul above,
With Christ, my Lord, eternally
  To share Thy glory and Thy love!
Then comes it right and well to me,
When, where, and how my death shall be.

66.   C. M.

1 LORD, it belongs not to my care,
    Whether I die or live;
  To love and serve Thee is my share,
    And this thy grace must give.

2 If life be long, I will be glad,
    That I may long obey;
  If short—yet why should I be sad
    To soar to endless day?

3 Come, Lord, when grace has made me
      meet
    Thy blessed face to see;
  For, if thy work on earth be sweet,
    What will thy glory be?

4 Then shall I end my sad complaints,
    And weary, sinful days,
And join with the triumphant saints
    That sing Jehovah's praise.

5 My knowledge of that life is small,
    The eye of faith is dim;
But 't is enough that Christ knows all,
    And I shall be with Him.

167.   P. M.

1 When the spark of life is waning,
    Weep not for me.
When the languid eye is straining,
    Weep not for me.
When the feeble pulse is ceasing,
Start not at its swift decreasing;
'T is the fettered soul's releasing;
    Weep not for me.

2 When the pangs of death assail me,
    Weep not for me.
Christ is mine—he will not fail me;
    Weep not for me.
Yes, though sin and doubt endeavor
From his love my soul to sever,
Jesus is my strength for ever!
    Weep not for me.

Dying and Death.

168.   8s and 7s.

1 When the soul, on wings upsoaring,
   Triumphs o'er its last dread foe;
And, the Saviour's love adoring,
   To its heavenly rest doth go;
Once so trembling, weak, and fearful,
   Oft it falter'd in the race,
Now rejoicing, glad, and cheerful,
   Dying hours have dying grace.

2 Fear not, then, when foes assail thee,
   Fear not when the night is dark,
God's sure promise cannot fail thee,
   He will guide thy trembling bark;
He who once hath died to win thee,
   Will thy every want supply:
He in time will plant within thee
   Grace to live and grace to die.

169.   11s.

1 Farewell, my dear brethren, the time is at hand
   That we must be parted from this social band:
Our several engagements now call us away,
   Our parting is needful, and we must obey.

2 Farewell, my dear brethren, farewell for a while,
We'll soon meet again, if kind Providence smile;
But when we are parted and scattered abroad,
We'll pray for each other, and wrestle with God.

3 Farewell, faithful soldiers, you'll soon be discharged,
The war will be ended, your treasures enlarged:
With shouting and singing, though Jordan may roar,
We'll enter fair Canaan, and stand on the shore.

4 Farewell, ye young converts, enlisted for war,
Sore trials await you, but Jesus is near:
Although you must travel the dark wilderness,
Your Captain's before you, he'll lead you to peace.

5 Farewell, faithful Christians, farewell, all around,
Perhaps we'll not meet till the last trump shall sound:
To meet you in glory I give you my hand,
Our Saviour to praise in the heavenly land.

Dying and Death.

170.   C. M.

1 Our sins, alas! how strong they be,
    And, like a raging flood,
  They break our duty, Lord, to thee.
    And force us from our God.

2 The waves of trouble, how they rise!
    How loud the tempests roar!
  But death shall land our weary souls
    Safe on the heavenly shore.

3 There to fulfil his sweet commands
    Our speedy feet shall move;
  No sin shall clog our winged zeal,
    Or cool our burning love.

4 There shall we ever sing, and tell
    The wonders of his grace,
  While heavenly raptures fire our hearts
    And smile in every face.

5 For ever his dear, sacred name
    Shall dwell upon our tongue,
  And Jesus and salvation be
    The close of every song.

THE SOLDIER'S DEATH SONG.
171.   12s and 11s.

1 I have fought the good fight, I have
    finished my race,
  And thee, O my Saviour, I soon shall
    embrace :

They may torture this body, my spirit is free,
And the billows of death shall but waft it to thee.

2 Let thy strength, Lord, but gird me —
thy smile be but mine,
And my soul on thy faithfulness firmly recline:
The cannon, the sword, or the shell I can dare,
And in transports expire, if my Jesus be there.

3 Did my Lord feel the scourge? Did the thorns pierce his brow?
In the darkness of death, on the cross did he bow?
All this didst thou suffer, my Saviour, for me;
Then, welcome the fetters that link me to thee.

4 United in sufferings—the promise is clear,
I shall with my Jesus in glory appear:
Out of great tribulation in triumph I go,
With my robe washed in blood, and made whiter than snow.

5 I go to my Saviour—I go to my God:
 I tread the same path my Redeemer once
   trod:
 Unworthy, my Jesus, unworthy am I,
 E'en to fall in thy cause—for thy truth
   e'en to die.

6 Lo! on my clear vision the seats of the
   blest
 Seem calmly to shine, and invite me to
   rest:
 Then, unshaken, my soul on the promise
   relies,
 "Though I die, I shall live—though I fall,
   I shall rise."

172.   P. M.

1 THERE is a happy land,
       Far, far away,
   Where saints in glory stand,
       Bright, bright as day;
   Oh, how they sweetly sing,
   Worthy is our Saviour King!
   Loud let his praises ring,
       Praise, praise for aye.

2 Come to that happy land,
       Come, come away;
   Why will ye doubting stand,
       Why still delay?

Oh! we shall happy be,
When, from sin and sorrow free,
Lord, we shall live with thee,
    Blest, blest for aye!

3 Bright, in that happy land,
    Beams every eye;
Kept by a Father's hand,
    Love cannot die:
Oh, then to glory run!
Be a crown and kingdom won;
And bright, above the sun,
    We reign for aye!

173.   7s.

1 High in yonder realms of light,
    Dwell the raptured saints above;
Far beyond our feeble sight,
    Happy in Immanuel's love:
Pilgrims in this vale of tears,
    Once they knew, like us below,
Gloomy doubts, distressing fears,
    Torturing pain, and heavy woe.

2 Oft the big, unbidden tear,
    Stealing down the furrowed cheek,
Told, in eloquence sincere,
    Tales of woe they could not speak.

But, these days of weeping o'er,
  Past this scene of toil and pain,
They shall feel distress no more,
  Never, never weep again.

'Mid the chorus of the skies,
  'Mid th' angelic lyres above,
Hark! their songs melodious rise,
  Songs of praise to Jesus' love.
Happy spirits ye are fled
  Where no grief can entrance find;
Lulled to rest the aching head,
  Soothed the anguish of the mind.

All is tranquil and serene,
  Calm and undisturbed repose;
There no cloud can intervene,
  There no angry tempest blows.
Every tear is wiped away,
  Sighs no more shall heave the breast,
Night is lost in endless day,
  Sorrow in eternal rest.

4.   C. M.

Come, Lord, and warm each languid heart,
  Inspire each lifeless tongue;
And let the joys of heaven impart
  Their influence to our song.

2 Sorrow, and pain, and every care,
   And discord there shall cease;
And perfect joy, and love sincere,
   Adorn the realms of peace.

3 The soul from sin for ever free,
   Shall mourn its power no more;
But, clothed in spotless purity,
   Redeeming love adore.

4 There on a throne how dazzling bright
   The exalted Saviour shines,
And beams ineffable delight
   On all the heavenly minds.

5 There shall the followers of the Lamb
   Join in immortal songs,
And endless honors to his name
   Employ their tuneful tongues.

6 Lord, tune our hearts to praise and love
   Our feeble notes inspire;
Till, in thy blissful courts above,
   We join the angelic choir.

175.   C. M.

1 Hail! sweetest, dearest tie that binds
   Our glowing hearts in one:
Hail! sacred hope that tunes our minds
   To joys before unknown.

It is the hope, the blissful hope,
  Which Jesus' grace has given:
The hope, when days and years are past,
  We all shall meet in heaven.

What though the surly winter blast
  May howl around our cot:
What though beneath an eastern sun
  Be cast our distant lot:
    We have the hope, etc.

No lingering look, no parting sigh,
  Our future meeting knows:
There friendship beams from every eye,
  And love immortal glows.
    We have the hope, etc.

3.   7s and 8s.

Jesus lives, and so shall I;
  Death! thy sting is gone for ever!
He, who deigned for me to die,
  Lives, the bands of death to sever.
He shall raise me with the just;
Jesus is my hope and trust.

Jesus lives, and by his grace
  Victory o'er my passions gaining,
I will cleanse my heart and ways,
  Ever to his glory living.
Weak he'll raise me from the dust;
Jesus is my hope and trust.

3 Jesus lives, and death is now
    But my entrance into glory.
  Courage! then, my soul, for thou
    Hast a crown of life before thee!
  Thou shalt find thy hopes were just;
  Jesus is the Christian's trust.

177.   L. M.

1 Let me be with thee where thou art,
    My Saviour, my eternal rest;
  Then only will this longing heart
    Be fully and for ever blest.

2 Let me be with thee where thou art,
    Thy unveiled glory to behold;
  Then only will this wandering heart
    Cease to be, false to thee, and cold.

3 Let me be with thee where thou art,
    Where spotless saints thy name adore;
  Then only will this sinful heart
    Be evil and defiled no more.

4 Let me be with thee where thou art,
    Where none can die, where none remove;
  There neither death nor life will part
    Me from thy presence and thy love.

78. P. M.

I 'm a pilgrim, and I 'm a stranger;
I can tarry but a night;
Do not detain me, for I am going
To where the rivers are ever flowing.

There the sunbeams are ever shining,
I am longing for the sight;
Within a country unknown and dreary,
I have been wand'ring, forlorn and weary.

Of the country to which I 'm going,
My Redeemer is the light;
There is no sorrow, nor any sighing,
Nor any sinning, nor any dying.
  I 'm a pilgrim, and I 'm a stranger,
  I can tarry but a night.

79. 8s and 7s.

WHEN we pass through yonder river,
  When we reach the farther shore,
There 's an end of war for ever;
  We shall see our foes no more:
All our conflicts then shall cease,
Followed by eternal peace.

2 After warfare, rest is pleasant,
  O how sweet the prospect is!
Though we toil and fight at present,
  Let us not repine at this:
Toil, and pain, and conflict past,
All endear repose at last.

3 When we gain the heavenly regions,
  When we touch the heavenly shore—
Blessed thought! no hostile legions
  Can alarm or trouble more;
Far beyond the reach of foes,
We shall dwell in sweet repose.

4 O that hope! how bright, how glorious.
  'T is his people's blest reward;
In the Saviour's strength victorious,
  They at length behold their Lord:
In his kingdom they shall rest,
In his love be fully blest.

180. S. M.

1 For ever with the Lord!
    Amen, so let it be:
  Life from the dead, is in that word,
    'T is immortality.

2 Here in the body pent,
    Absent from Him I roam,
  Yet nightly pitch my moving tent
    A day's march nearer home.

3 My Father's house on high,
 Home of my soul, how near
At times to faith's illumined eye
 Thy golden gates appear.

4 My thirsty spirit faints
 To reach the land I love,
The bright inheritance of saints,
 Jerusalem above.

31. P. M.

JOYFULLY, joyfully, onward I move,
Bound to the land of bright spirits above;
Angelic choristers sing as I come—
Joyfully, joyfully, haste to thy home!
Soon with my pilgrimage ended below,
Home to the land of bright spirits I go;
Pilgrim and stranger no more shall I roam;
Joyfully, joyfully, resting at home.

Friends, fondly cherished, have passed on before;
Waiting, they watch me approaching the shore;
Singing to cheer me through death's chilling gloom,
Joyfully, joyfully, haste to thy home.

Sounds of sweet melody fall on my e[ar]
Harps of the blessed, your voices I he[ar]
Rings with the harmony heaven's b[lue]
   dome—
Joyfully, joyfully, haste to thy home.

3 Death, with thy weapons of war lay
   low,
Strike, king of terrors! I fear not the blow
Jesus hath broken the bars of the tomb
Joyfully, joyfully, will I go home.
Bright with the morn of eternity's
Death shall be banished, his sceptre
   gone;
Joyfully, then, shall I witness his doom,
Joyfully, joyfully, safely at home.

182.   8s and 7s.

1 THERE is an hour of peaceful rest,
   To mourning wanderers given;
There is a joy for souls distressed,
A balm for every wounded breast,
   'T is found above—in heaven.

2 There is a home for weary souls,
   By sin and sorrow driven;
When tossed on life's tempestuous shoals
Where storms arise, and ocean rolls,
   And all is drear but heaven.

There faith lifts up her cheerful eye
To brighter prospects given;
And views the tempests passing by,
The evening shadows quickly fly,
And all serene in heaven.

There fragrant flowers, immortal, bloom,
And joys supreme are given;
There rays divine disperse the gloom;
Beyond the confines of the tomb
Appears the dawn of heaven.

183. 11s.

1 I'M weary of straying—O fain would I rest
In that far distant land of the pure and the blest,
Where sin can no longer her blandishments spread,
And tears and temptations for ever are fled.

2 I'm weary of hoping—where hope is untrue,
As fair, but as fleeting as morning's bright dew:
I long for that land whose bless'd promise alone
Is changeless and sure as eternity's throne.
12

3 I'm weary of sighing o'er sorrows of earth,
  O'er joy's glowing visions that fade at their birth—
  O'er the pangs of the loved, which we cannot assuage—
  O'er the blightings of youth, and the weakness of age.

4 I'm weary of loving what passes away—
  The sweetest, the dearest, alas! may not stay;
  I long for that land where those partings are o'er,
  And death and the tomb can divide hearts no more.

5 I'm weary, my Saviour, of grieving thy love:
  O when shall I rest in thy presence above?
  I'm weary—but O never let me repine:
  Thy word, and thy love, and thy promise are mine.

184.   6s and 7s.

1 WILL that not joyful be,
  When we walk by faith no more,
  When the Lord we loved before,
As Brother-man we see;
  When he welcomes us above,
  When we share his smile of love,
Will that not joyful be?

Heaven.

2 Will that not joyful be,
　When to meet us rise and come
　All our buriëd treasures home,
A gladsome company?
　When our arms embrace again
　Those we mourned so long in vain,
Will that not joyful be?

3 Will that not joyful be,
　When we hear what none can tell,
　And the ringing chorus swell
Of angels' melody?
　When we join their songs of praise,
　Hallelujahs with them raise,
Will that not joyful be?

4 Yes! that will joyful be;
　Let the world her gifts recall;
　There is bitterness in all;
Her joys are vanity!
　Courage, dear ones of my heart!
　Though it grieves us here to part,
There we shall joyful be!

185.　　　　C. M.

1 JERUSALEM, my happy home,
　Name ever dear to me!
When shall my labors have an end,
　In joy, and peace, and thee?

2 When shall these eyes thy Heaven-built
  walls
   And pearly gates behold?
  Thy bulwarks, with salvation strong.
   And streets of shining gold?
3 There happier bowers than Eden's bloom.
   Nor sin nor sorrow know:
  Blest seats, through rude and stormy
    scenes,
   I onward press to you.
4 Why should I shrink at pain and woe,
   Or feel, at death, dismay?
  I've Canaan's goodly land in view.
   And realms of endless day.
5 Apostles, martyrs, prophets there
   Around my Saviour stand;
  And soon my friends in Christ below
   Will join the glorious band.
6 Jerusalem, my happy home,
   My soul still pants for thee;
  Then shall my labors have an end
   When I thy joys shall see.

186.   C. M.
1 On Jordan's stormy banks I stand,
   And cast a wishful eye
  To Canaan's fair and happy land,
   Where my possessions lie.

Heaven. 181

2 O the transporting, rapturous scene,
    That rises to my sight:
Sweet fields arrayed in living green,
    And rivers of delight.

3 There generous fruits, that never fail,
    On trees immortal grow;
There rocks, and hills, and brooks, and vales
    With milk and honey flow.

4 On all those wide-extended plains
    Shines one eternal day;
There God the Son for ever reigns,
    And scatters night away.

5 No chilling winds nor poisonous breath
    Can reach that healthful shore:
Sickness and sorrow, pain and death,
    Are felt and feared no more.

187.　　　　C. M.

1 THERE is a land of pure delight
    Where saints immortal reign;
Infinite day excludes the night,
    And pleasures banish pain.

2 There everlasting spring abides,
    And never-withering flowers;
Death, like a narrow sea, divides
    This heavenly land from ours.

3 Sweet fields beyond the swelling flood
   Stand dressed in living green;
 So to the Jews old Canaan stood,
   While Jordan rolled between.

4 But timorous mortals start and shrink
   To cross this narrow sea;
 And linger, shivering on the brink,
   And fear to launch away!

5 Oh! could we make our doubts remove,
   Those gloomy doubts that rise,
 And see the Canaan that we love
   With unbeclouded eyes:

6 Could we but climb where Moses stood,
   And view the landscape o'er,
 Not Jordan's stream, nor death's cold flood,
   Should fright us from the shore.

188. C. M.

1 GIVE me the wings of faith, to rise
   Within the veil, and see
 The saints above, how great their joys,
   How bright their glories be.

2 Once they were mourning here below,
   And wet their couch with tears;
 They wrestled hard, as we do now,
   With sins, and doubts, and fears.

Heaven.

3 I ask them whence their victory came;
  They, with united breath,
Ascribe their contest to the Lamb,
  Their triumph to his death.

4 They marked the footsteps that He trod,
  His zeal inspired their breast:
And, following their incarnate God,
  Possessed the promised rest.

189.   C. M.

1 Thou dear Redeemer, dying Lamb,
  We love to hear of thee;
No music 's like thy charming name.
  Nor half so sweet can be.

2 O may we ever hear thy voice
  In mercy to us speak;
And in our Priest we will rejoice,
  Thou great Melchisedec.

3 Our Jesus shall be still our theme,
  While in this world we stay;
We 'll sing our Jesus' lovely name
  When all things else decay.

4 When we appear in yonder cloud,
  With all the favor'd throng,
Then will we sing more sweet, more loud.
  And Christ shall be our song.

190. 8s and 7s—peculiar.

1 When in this world of grief and pain
   We from our friends must sever,
'T is sweet to look beyond this scene,
   Where we shall meet for ever.

2 Though time and absence may estrange
   The hearts once knit together,
Yet severed friends shall meet again,
   To part no more for ever.

3 Where partings ne'er shall sink the heart,
   Where sorrow enters never,
And sin no longer can defile
   Those whom we love for ever.

4 Sweet thought! this earth is not our rest,
   Where troubles crowd together;
But one with Jesus we shall dwell,
   And reign with him for ever.

191. 11s.

1 An alien from God, and a stranger to grace,
   I 've wandered through earth, its gay pleasures to trace;
In the pathway of sin I continued to roam,
Unmindful, alas! that it led me from home.
   Home, home, sweet, sweet, home,
     O Saviour, direct me to heaven, my home.

The pleasures of earth I have seen fade away.
They bloom for a season, but soon they decay:
But pleasures more lasting in Jesus are given,
Salvation on earth, and a mansion in heaven.
  Home, home, sweet, sweet home,
  The saints in those mansions are ever at home.

Allure me no longer, ye false, glowing charms!
The Saviour invites me, I'll go to his arms:
At the banquet of mercy I hear there is room,
O there may I feast with his children at home!
  Home, home, sweet, sweet home,
  O Jesus, conduct me to heaven, my home.

The days of my exile are passing away.
The time is approaching when Jesus will say,

"Well done, faithful servant, triumphant come,
And dwell in my presence for ever home."
Home, home, sweet, sweet home,
O there I shall rest with the Saviour at home.

192. 8s and 7s.

1 Death shall not destroy my comfort,
Christ shall guide me through the gloom
Down he'll send some heavenly convoy,
To convey my spirit home:
Jordan's streams shall ne'er o'erflow m
While my Saviour's by my side:
Canaan, Canaan lies before me,
Rise and cross the swelling tide.

2 See the happy spirits waiting
On the banks beyond the stream,
Sweet responses still repeating—
Jesus, Jesus is their theme:
See, they whisper! hark! they call me—
Sister spirit, come away!
Lo, I come! earth can't contain me!
Hail, ye realms of endless day!

Smiling angels now surround me,
  Troops resplendent fill the skies,
Glory shining all around me,
  While my towering spirit flies:
Jesus, clad in dazzling splendor,
  Now, methinks, appears in view:
Brethren, could you see my Jesus,
  You would serve and love him too.

HERE AND THERE.
7s.

When the shaded pilgrim land
  Fades before my closing eye,
Then reveal'd on either hand
  Heaven's own scenery shall lie;
Then the veil of flesh shall fall,
Now concealing, darkening all.

Heavenly landscapes, calmly bright,
  Life's pure river murmuring low,
Forms of loveliness and light
  Lost to earth long time ago;
Yes, mine own, lamented long,
Shine amid the angel throng!

When upon my wearied ear
  Earth's last echoes faintly die,
Then shall angel harps draw near—
  All the chorus of the sky;
Long-hushed voices blend again,
Sweetly, in that

Heaven.

1 When this aching heart shall rest,
    All its busy pulses o'er,
From her mortal robes undresssed,
    Shall my spirit upward soar.
Then shall unimagined joy
All my thoughts and powers employ

5 Here devotion's healing balm
    Often came to soothe my breast;
Hours of deep and holy calm,
    Earnests of eternal rest.
But the bliss was here unknown,
Which shall there be all my own!

6 Jesus reigns, the Life, the Sun
    Of that wondrous world above;
All the clouds and storms are gone,
    All is light, and all is love.
All earth's shadows melt away
In the blaze of perfect day.

194. P. M.

1 Oh! haste away, my brethren dear,
    And come to Canaan's shore;
We'll meet and sing for ever there,
    When all our toils are o'er.

Heaven.

h! that will be joyful, joyful, joyful,
Oh! that will be joyful,
To meet to part no more,
To meet to part no more,
On Canaan's happy shore;
And sing the everlasting song
With those who 've gone before.

ow sweet to hear the hallowed theme
  That saints shall ever sing;
o hear their voices all proclaim,
  "Salvation to the King."
Oh! that will be, etc.

Around His throne, all clothed in white,
  Will all His saints appear,
And, shining in His glory bright,
  Will see our Saviour there.
Oh! that will be, etc.

Through heaven the shouts of angels
  When sons to God are born:
Oh! what a company will sing
  On the millennial morn.
Oh! that will be, etc.

Through one eternal day we'll sing,
  And bless His sacred name,
With hallelujah to the King,
  And "Worthy is the Lamb."
Oh! that will be, etc.

195. 6s and 5s.

1 When shall we meet again?
    Meet ne'er to sever?
When will peace wreathe her chain
    Round us for ever?
Our hearts will ne'er repose,
Safe from each blast that blows,
In this dark vale of woes—
    Never—no, never!

2 When shall love freely flow
    Pure as life's river?
When shall sweet friendship glow
    Changeless for ever?
Where joys celestial thrill,
Where bliss each heart shall fill
And fears of parting chill
    Never—no, never!

Up to that world of light
    Take us, dear Saviour:
May we all there unite,
    Happy for ever:
Where kindred spirits dwell,
There may our music swell,
And time our joys dispel
    Never—no, never!

4 Soon shall we meet again—
    Meet ne'er to sever:
Soon will peace wreathe her chain
    Round us for ever:
Our hearts will then repose
Secure from worldly woes;
Our songs of praise shall close
    Never—no, never!

96.   S. M.

And is there, Lord, a rest
    For weary souls designed,
Where not a care shall stir the breast,
    Or sorrow entrance find?

Is there a blissful home,
    Where kindred minds shall meet,
And live, and love, nor ever roam
    From that serene retreat?

Are there bright, happy fields,
    Where naught that blooms shall die;
Where each new scene fresh pleasure
    yields,
    And healthful breezes sigh?

Are there celestial streams,
    Where living waters glide,
With murmurs sweet as angel dreams,
    And flowery banks beside?

5 For ever blessed they
   Whose joyful feet shall stand—
While endless ages waste away—
   Amid that glorious land!

6 My soul would thither tend,
   While toilsome years are given;
Then let me, gracious God, ascend
   To sweet repose in heaven!

197. C. M.

1 FAR from these narrow scenes of night
   Unbounded glories rise,
And realms of infinite delight,
   Unknown to mortal eyes.

2 Fair, distant land! could mortal eyes
   But half its charms explore,
How would our spirits long to rise,
   And dwell on earth no more!

3 No cloud those blissful regions know—
   Realms ever bright and fair!
For sin, the source of mortal woe,
   Can never enter there.

4 Oh, may the heavenly prospect fire
   Our hearts with ardent love!
Till wings of faith, and strong desire,
   Bear every thought above.

Heaven.

5 Prepare us, Lord, by grace divine,
   For Thy bright courts on high;
 Then bid our spirits rise and join
   The chorus of the sky.

198.   7s and 6s.

1 SOLDIERS, by our Lord's command,
 Marching to the happy land,
 Soon we'll join the glorious band
   In yon bright world of light.
Chorus—I believe I shall be there,
   I believe I shall be there,
   I believe I shall be there,
     And walk with Him in white.

2 Thousands are already there,
 Ranging through the regions fair,
 Crowns of righteousness they wear
   In yon bright world of light.
           Chorus.

3 We shall reach the peaceful shore,
 Storms and tempests shall be o'er,
 We shall praise Him evermore
   In yon bright world of light.
           Chorus.

4 There we shall for ever dwell,
 Make the heavenly music swell;
 Time shall ne'er our joys dispel
   In yon bright world of light.
           Chorus.

Heaven.

5 We shall know as we are known,
Heirs to God's eternal throne,
Glory be to God alone
  In yon bright world of light.
         Chorus.

6 Soon the trump shall bid us rise,
Take possession of the prize,
Welcome! welcome to the skies!
  In yon bright world of light.
         Chorus.

199.   6s and 8s.

1 O SING to me of heaven,
    When I am called to die;
  Sing songs of holy ecstacy,
    To waft my soul on high.

2 When cold and sluggish drops
    Roll off my marble brow,
  Break forth in songs of joyfulness,
    Let heaven begin below.

3 When the last moment comes,
    O watch my dying face,
  And catch the bright seraphic gleam
    That o'er each feature plays.

4 Then to my raptured ear
    Let one sweet song be given,
  Let Jesus cheer me last on earth,
    And greet me first in heaven.

5 Close then my sightless eyes,
  And lay me down to rest,
And clasp my cold and icy hands
  Upon my lifeless breast.

6 Then round my senseless clay
  Assemble those I love,
And sing of heaven, delightful heaven,
  My glorious home above.

200. L. M.

1 BEFORE Jehovah's awful throne,
  Ye nations, bow with sacred joy;
Know that the Lord is God alone;
  He can create, and he destroy.

2 His sovereign power, without our aid,
  Made us of clay, and form'd us men;
And, when like wandering sheep we stray'd,
  He brought us to his fold again.

3 We are his people, we his care,
  Our souls, and all our mortal frame;
What lasting honors shall we rear,
  Almighty Maker, to thy Name?

4 We'll crowd thy gates with thankful songs,
  High as the heaven our voices raise;
And earth with her ten thousand tongues,
  Shall fill thy courts with sounding praise.

5 Wide as the world is thy command,
    Vast as eternity thy love;
Firm as a rock thy truth must stand,
    When rolling years shall cease to move.

201.   L. M.—6-line.

1 From stern oppression's haughty land
    Our fathers crossed the boisterous wave;
A patient, firm, and patriot band;
    Thou, God of battles, mad'st them brave;
O make us ever blest and free,
A land of peace and liberty.

2 To thee, their steadfast, suppliant eyes
    Were raised, 'mid war and dread alarm;
O God of battles, from the skies
    Thy mercy sent the conquering arm;
Still guard our freedom, rights, and fame,
While we exalt thy holy name.

3 Here, we the children of the tree,
    Now gladly chant the joyful song,
And own our boundless debt to thee,
    Which time shall gladly bear along;
Be this our cheering battle-cry,
For God, for home, for liberty!

202. C. M.

O Lord, our fathers oft have told
  In our attentive ears,
Thy wonders in their days performed,
  And in more ancient years.

2 'T was not their courage nor their sword
  To them salvation gave;
'T was not their number nor their strength
  That did our country save.

3 But thy right hand, thy powerful arm,
  Whose succor they implored;
Thy providence protected them,
  Who thy great name adored.

4 As thee their God our fathers owned,
  So thou art still our King;
O therefore, as thou didst to them,
  To us deliverance bring.

5 To thee the glory we ascribe,
  From whom salvation came;
In God, our shield, we will rejoice,
  And ever bless thy name.

203. 8s, 7s, and 4s.

1 Hallelujah! victory! victory!
    Lift the conqueror's song on high!
  Jesus drives the foe before us,
    Lo, our foes before us fly,
      Hallelujah,
  Now our joyful hearts reply.

Our Country—Praise

2 Long and fierce has been the conflict;
　Long the issue hung in doubt;
Though united all their forces,
　All were foiled and put to rout:
　　Hallelujah!
Raise to heaven the rapturous shout.

3 Hallelujah—to our Leader!
　Let the triumph widely spread,
'T was his strong, all-conquering banner
　Struck the raging foe with dread;
　　Hallelujah!
To our glorious, living Head!

204.　　　　6s and 4s.

1 My country, 't is of thee,
　Sweet land of liberty,
　　Of thee I sing:
Land where my fathers died,
Land of the Southron's pride,
From every mountain side
　　Let freedom ring!

2 My native country, thee—
　Land of the noble, free—
　　Thy name I love:
I love thy rocks and rills,
Thy woods and templed hills;
My heart with rapture thrills
　　Like those above.

3 Let music swell the breeze,
  And ring from all the trees
    Sweet freedom's song!
  Let mortal tongues awake:
  Let all that breathe partake;
  Let rocks their silence break—
    The sound prolong.

4 Our fathers' God! to thee,
  Author of liberty,
    To thee we sing:
  Still may our land be bright
  With freedom's holy light;
  Protected by thy might,
    Great God, our King!

205. P. M.

1 GIVE thanks to God most high,
  The universal Lord;
The sovereign King of kings:
  And be his grace adored.
    His power and grace
  Are still the same;
  And let his name
    Have endless praise.

2 He smote the first-born sons,
  The flower of Egypt, dead;
And thence his chosen tribes
  With joy and glory led.

Thy mercy, Lord,
Shall still endure;
And ever sure
Abide thy word.

3 His power and lifted rod
 Cleft the Red sea in two;
And for his people made
 A wondrous passage through.
  His power and grace
  Are still the same;
  And let his name
  Have endless praise.

4 Give thanks aloud to God,
 To God, the heavenly King;
And let the spacious earth
 His works and glories sing.
  Thy mercy, Lord,
  To us secure,
  And ever sure
  Abide thy word.

206. *Air*—"God save the King."

1 GOD of the brave and free,
 Father of all, to Thee
  Our voice we raise;
For all thy blessings shown,
For deeds of mercy done,
Thy guardian care we own;
  Accept our praise.

2 Now in our deep distress
  Oh! deign our cause to bless,
    And hear our prayer;
  Now, while the din of war,
  And the loud cannon's roar
  Resound from shore to shore,
    Be ever near.

3 Oh! shield us in the day
  Of battle's fierce array,
    Let none despair;
  May all with heart and hand,
  A firm united band,
  Resolve to take their stand,
    Nor danger fear.

4 Protect us with Thy arm,
  Keep us from every harm,
    Our cause maintain;
  May we victorious be,
  From rude invaders free,
  Conquerors by land and sea,
    And peace regain.

5 Then, when our land shall be
  Restored to liberty,
    Our God, the Lord;
  Peace and prosperity
  When all our borders see,
  May we a nation be,
    Built on Thy word.

207. L. M.

1 Sovereign of all the worlds above,
   Thy glory, with unclouded rays,
 Shines through the realms of light and
     love,
   Inspiring angels with thy praise.

2 Thy power we own, thy grace adore;
   Who deign'st to visit man below;
 And in affliction's darkest hour
   The humble shall thy mercy know.

3 These Southern states at thy command
   Rose from dependence and distress;
 And, 'stablished by thy mighty hand,
   Millions shall join thy name to bless.

4 We'll praise thy name, eternal King;
   We'll speak the wonders of thy love:
 With grateful hearts our tribute bring,
   And emulate the hosts above.

5 Be thou, then, Lord, our guardian God;
   Preserve these States from every foe;
 From party rage, from scenes of blood,
   From sin, and every cause of woe.

6 Here may the great Redeemer reign,
   Display his grace and saving power;
 Here liberty and truth maintain,
   Till empires fall to rise no more.

208. C. M.

1 Our land, O Lord, with songs of praise
    Shall in thy strength rejoice;
  And, blest with thy salvation, raise
    To heaven their cheerful voice.

2 Thy sure defence through nations round
    Has spread our glorious name;
  And our successful actions crown'd
    With dignity and fame.

3 Then let our land on God alone
    For timely aid rely;
  His mercy, which adorns his throne,
    Shall all our wants supply.

4 Yes, righteous Lord, thy stubborn foes
    Shall feel thy dreadful power;
  Thy vengeful arm shall find out those
    Who would thy saints devour.

5 Now, Lord, thy wondrous power declare,
    And thus exalt thy fame;
  While we glad songs of praise prepare
    For thine almighty name.

209. C. M.

1 To thine almighty arm we owe
    The triumphs of the day;
  Thy terrors, Lord, confound the foe,
    And melt their strength away.

2 'T is by thy aid our troops prevail,
  And break united powers;
 Or burn their boasted fleets, or scale
  The proudest of their towers.

3 How have we chas'd them through the field,
  And trod them to the ground;
 While thy salvation was *our* shield
  They no safe shelter found!

4 In vain to vengeful heaven they cry—
  They perish in their blood.
 Where is a rock so great, so high,
  So powerful, as our God?

5 The Rock of Israel ever lives,
  His name be ever blest;
 'T is his own arm the victory gives,
  And gives his people rest.

210. 11s and 10s.

1 DAUGHTER of Zion, awake from thy sadness;
  Awake, for thy foes shall oppress thee no more;
 Bright o'er thy hills dawns the day-star of gladness;
  Arise, for the night of thy sorrow is o'er.

2 Strong are thy foes, but the arm that
    subdues them,
  And scatters their legions, is mightier
    far;
  They 'll flee, like the chaff, from the
    scourge that pursues them;
  Vain, vain are their steeds and their
    chariots of war.

3 Daughter of Zion, the Power that still
    saves thee,
  Extolled with the harp and the tim-
    brel should be;
  Shout, for the foe is destroyed that en-
    slaved thee,
  The oppressor is vanquished, and Zion
    is free.

211. C. M.

1 SNATCHED, Lord, from danger and from
    death,
  My thankful voice I raise;
  To laud his name who spares my breath,
    In grateful hymns of praise.

2 As on destruction's brink aghast
    I stood with panting breath,
  And thought each moment was my last,
    And looked for instant death;

3 In that dread hour of deep despair
　　I raised my earnest cry;
　My Saviour heard the broken prayer,
　　His hand unseen was nigh.

4 For ever thy bless'd Name I'll praise,
　　Who saved me from above;
　And my spared life and rescued days
　　Shall glorify thy love.

212.　　　　C. M.

1 In thee, great God! with songs of praise
　　Our favored States rejoice;
　And, blest with thy salvation, raise
　　To heaven their cheerful voice.

2 In deep distress, our injured land
　　Implored thy power to save;
　For victory prayed—thy powerful hand
　　The glorious blessing gave.

3 On thee, in want, in woe, or pain,
　　Our hearts alone rely;
　Our rights thy mercy will maintain,
　　And all our wants supply.

4 Still, Lord! thy wondrous power declare,
　　Exalt thy glorious Name;
　While we glad songs of praise prepare,
　　To celebrate thy fame.

213.   L. P. M.

1 With grateful hearts, with joyful tongues,
To God we raise united songs;
　His power and mercy we proclaim:
Through every age, Oh! may we own
Jehovah here has fixed his throne—
　And triumph in his mighty Name.

2 Long as the moon her course shall run,
Or men behold the circling sun,
　Lord! in our land, support thy reign;
Crown her just counsels with success,
With truth and peace her borders bless,
　And all her sacred rights maintain.

214.   C. M.

1 Thy mighty arm, O God, was nigh
　When we our foes assailed;
'T was thou who raised our honors high,
　And o'er their hosts prevailed.

2 The thundering horse, the martial band,
　Without thine aid were vain;
For victory flies at thy command
　To crown the bright campaign.

3 How didst Thou break the spear and
　　shield,
　The battle and the bow!
How to thy glorious might did yield
　The vaunting, boastful foe!

4 There was the ruthless spoiler spoiled;
 And in promiscuous heap—
Their artful skill and prowess foiled—
 The proud in death did sleep;

5 O Lord when thy rebuke is heard,
 Rider and horse expire;
Thou, God of Jacob, shalt be feared,
 Our foes have felt thine ire.

215.   6s and 8s.

1 "Not unto us, O Lord,
 Not unto us," be praise!
But to Thy glorious name
 Our grateful songs we raise.
The Lord Jehovah is our trust,
For we His creatures are but dust.

2 Our souls with grief were bowed,
  Our sins had brought us low;
 No human help was nigh,
  No refuge did we know.
To God we cried, in deep distress,
And He hath kindly deigned to bless.

3 Our foes against us rose,
  And compassed us around,
 They purposed to destroy,
  But we deliverance found.
The Lord of hosts was on our side,
And humbled all the sons of pride.

4 Their marshalled hosts drew nigh
   In long and proud array,
We had no might nor power
   To conquer in the fray:
Our hope was in the Lord Most High,
And now His grace we magnify.

5 O nation blest of God!
   His power and goodness own,
Ascribe to Him the praise,
   Who hath the victory won.
We give Thee thanks, Almighty King,
Accept the homage which we bring.

DOXOLOGY.

Oh praise God's Triune Name!
   Extol His wondrous power!
With reverence and with awe,
   This mystery adore!
"His kingdom ruleth over all,"
Let all the nations prostrate fall!

216.   C. M.

1 THE Lord appears our helper now;
   Nor is our faith afraid
What all the sons of earth can do,
   Since heaven affords its aid.

Our Country—

2 'T is safer, Lord, to hope in thee,
    And have our God our friend,
Than trust in men of high degree,
    And on their power depend.

3 Like bees our foes beset us round,
    A fierce and deadly swarm;
But all their rage we shall confound
    By Thine almighty arm.

4 'T is through the Lord each heart is strong;
    Through thee our souls rejoice:
While thy salvation is our song
    How cheerful is our voice!

217.   6s and 4s.

1 Our land, with mercies crowned,
  This wide, enchanted ground,
    O God, is thine:
Our fathers knew thy name;
The trophies of their fame—
Our heritage—proclaim
    A power divine.

2 Still, Lord, defend the right,
  In freedom's fearful fight,
    From all its foes.
A nation now create,
And lead its marches great,
And build its pillared state,
    And grant repose.

Confidence and Hope.

3 Dear native land! rejoice;
Raise thou thy virgin voice
    To God on high;
From all thy hills and bays,
From all thy homes and ways,
Let symphonies and praise
    Ascend the sky.

4 And Thou, Almighty one,
At whose eternal throne
    She bows the knee;
In all the coming time,
Bless thou this favored clime,
And may her deeds sublime
    Be hymns to thee!

218. L. C. M.

Gustavus Adolphus' Battle Song, A. D., 1631.

1 FEAR not, O little flock, the foe
Who madly seeks your overthrow;
    Dread not his rage and power:
What though your courage sometimes faints,
His seeming triumph o'er God's saints
    Lasts but a little hour.

Our Country—

2 Be of good cheer; your cause belongs
  To him who can avenge your wrongs,
    Leave it to him, our Lord;
  Though hidden yet from all our eyes,
  He sees the Gideon who shall rise
    To save us, and his WORD.

3 As true as God's own Word is true
  Nor earth, nor hell, with all their crew,
    Against us shall prevail;
  A jest and byword they are grown:
  God is with us, we are his own,
    Our victory cannot fail.

4 Amen, Lord Jesus, grant our prayer!
  Great Captain, now thine arm make bare.
    Fight for us once again.
  So shall thy saints and martyrs raise
  A mighty chorus to thy praise,
    World without end—Amen.

219.   *8s and 7s.*

1 BE not dismay'd, thou little flock,
  Although the foe's fierce battle shock
    Loud on all sides assail thee:
  Though o'er thy fall they laugh secure,
  Their triumph can not long endure;
    Let not thy courage fail thee.

2 Thy cause is God's—go at His call,
　And to His hand commit thy all;
　　Fear thou no ill impending:
　His Gideon shall arise for thee,
　God's Word and people manfully
　　In God's own time defending.

3 Our hope is sure in Jesus' might;
　Against themselves the godless fight,
　　Themselves, not us, distressing;
　Shame and contempt their lot shall be;
　God is with us, with Him are we:
　　To us belongs His blessing.

220.   C. M.

1 'Tis faith supports my feeble soul,
　　In times of deep distress;
　When storms arise and billows roll,
　　Great God, I trust thy grace.

2 Thy powerful arm still bears me up,
　　Whatever griefs befall;
　Thou art my life, my joy, my hope,
　　And thou my all in all.

3 Bereft of friends, beset with foes,
　　With dangers all around,
　To thee I all my fears disclose,
　　In thee my help is found.

4 In every want, in every strait,
　To thee alone I fly;
When other comforters depart,
　Thou art for ever nigh.

221.　　　L. M.

1 Here at thy cross, incarnate God,
　I lay my soul beneath thy love:
Beneath the droppings of thy blood,
　Jesus, nor shall it e'er remove.

2 Not all that tyrants think or say,
　With rage and lightning in their eyes,
Nor hell shall fright my heart away,
　Should hell with all its legions rise.

3 Should worlds conspire to drive me thence,
　Moveless and firm this heart should lie;
Resolved, for that 's my last defence,
　If I must perish, there to die.

4 Yes, I 'm secure beneath thy blood,
　And all my foes shall lose their aim;
Hosanna to my Saviour God,
　And my best honors to his name.

22.   7s and 6s.

1 To the hills I lift mine eyes,
　　The everlasting hills;
Streaming thence in fresh supplies
　　My soul the Spirit feels:
Will he not his help afford?
　　Help, while yet I ask, is given:
God comes down—the God and Lord
　　That made both earth and heaven.

2 Faithful soul, pray always; pray,
　　And still in God confide;
He thy feeble steps shall stay,
　　Nor suffer thee to slide;
Lean on thy Redeemer's breast;
　　He thy quiet spirit keeps;
Rest in him, securely rest;
　　Thy watchman never sleeps.

3 Neither sin, nor earth, nor hell,
　　Thy keeper can surprise;
Careless slumbers cannot steal
　　On his all-seeing eyes;
He is Israel's sure defence;
　　Israel all his care shall prove;
Kept by watchful Providence,
　　And ever-waking love.

4 See the Lord, thy keeper, stand
    Omnipotently near:
Lo! he holds thee by thy hand,
    And banishes thy fear;
Shadows with his wings thy head:
    Guards from all impending harms:
Round thee and beneath are spread
    The everlasting arms.

5 Christ shall bless thy going out,
    Shall bless thy coming in;
Kindly compass thee about,
    Till thou art saved from sin;
Like thy spotless Master, thou,
    Filled with wisdom, love, and power;
Holy, pure, and perfect, now,
    Henceforth, and evermore.

223.   L. M.—6-line.

1 THE Lord's my banner! forth I go,
And dread no danger, fear no foe;
Though death, though hell beset my path,
I scorn their power, I brave their wrath;
Where'er I turn, whate'er betide,
My Lord shall combat by my side!

2 The Lord's my banner! Grief may low'r,
Or joy may gild the passing hour;
Alike in sunshine or in rain
My Captain shall his succor deign;
Alike I'll serve and trust my Lord;
His grace my shield, his word my sword!

The Lord's my banner! forward still
I press, obedient to his will;
The toils, the sufferings of my lot
In Christ's dear presence all forgot;
My only wish to find him nigh,
With him to live, in him to die!

The Lord's my banner! round my tomb
No wreath may twine, no cypress bloom;
No friend, no child may linger near,
To drop the tributary tear;
Yet there my gracious Lord shall wave
His blood-red banner o'er my grave!

24.   8s and 6s.

God is our refuge in distress—
Our safeguard in the wilderness,
    Our shelter from the storm;
Though winds and waves a conflict make,
Though earth's foundations reel and shake,
    We need not feel alarm.

A peaceful river softly flows
In tranquil streams, to gladden those
    Who put their trust in God;
Within his holy place they feel
The comfort of his presence still,
    While oceans roll abroad.

3 What though our foemen madly rage,
   And with us in fierce war engage?
      When God sends forth his voice
   He makes the glittering spear to bend,
   Sends peace to earth's remotest end,
      And bids the world rejoice.

4 Be still, and know that he is God;
   He rules the world with iron rod,
      And sits enthroned above;
   He dwells with those who own His name,
   The God of Jacob still the same,
      The God of peace and love.

225. S. M.

1 ARISE, ye saints, arise!
    The Lord our leader is;
   The foe before his banner flies,
    For victory is his.

2 Lead on, almighty Lord,
    Lead on to victory!
   Encouraged by the bright reward,
    With joy we'll follow thee.

3 We'll follow thee, our Guide,
    Our Saviour, and our King;
   We'll follow thee, through grace supplied
    From heaven's eternal spring.

4 We hope to see the day
    When all our toils shall cease;
When we shall cast our arms away,
    And dwell in endless peace.

5 This hope supports us here,
    It makes our burdens light;
'T will serve our drooping hearts to cheer
    Till faith shall end in sight;

6 Till, of the prize possessed,
    We hear of war no more;
And, oh! sweet thought! for ever rest
    On yonder peaceful shore!

226.   S. M.

1 In Zion God is known
    A refuge in distress;
How bright has his salvation shone
    Through all her palaces!

2 When kings against her join'd,
    And saw the Lord was there,
In wild confusion of the mind
    They fled with hasty fear.

3 When navies, tall and proud,
    Attempt to spoil our peace,
He sends his tempest roaring loud,
    And sinks them in the seas.

4 Oft have our fathers told,
   Our eyes have often seen,
How well our God secures the fold
   Where his own sheep have been.

5 In ev'ry new distress
   We'll to his house repair;
We'll think upon his wondrous grace
   And seek deliv'rance there.

227. C. M.

1 God moves in a mysterious way
   His wonders to perform:
He plants his footsteps in the sea,
   And rides upon the storm.

2 Ye fearful saints, fresh courage take
   The clouds ye so much dread
Are big with mercy, and shall break
   In blessings on your head.

3 Judge not the Lord by feeble sense,
   But trust him for his grace;
Behind a frowning providence
   He hides a smiling face.

4 His purposes will ripen fast,
   Unfolding every hour;
The bud may have a bitter taste,
   But sweet will be the flower.

Confidence and Hope.

5 Blind unbelief is sure to err,
    And scan his work in vain;
God is his own interpreter,
    And he will make it plain.

228.   L. M.

1 My spirit looks to God alone:
My rock and refuge is his throne;
In all my fears, in all my straits,
My soul on his salvation waits.

2 Trust him, ye saints, in all your ways,
Pour out your hearts before his face;
When helpers fail, and foes invade,
God is our all-sufficient aid.

3 Once has his awful voice declared,
Once and again my ears have heard
"All power is his eternal due;
He must be feared and trusted too."

229.   C. M.

1 O God of Bethel, by whose hand
    Thy people still are fed;
Who through this weary pilgrimage
    Hast all our fathers led;

2 Our vows, our prayers, we now present
    Before thy throne of grace:
God of our fathers, be the God
    Of their succeeding race.

Our Country—

3 Through each perplexing path of life
   Our wandering footsteps guide;
Give us each day our daily bread,
   And raiment fit provide.

4 O spread thy covering wings around,
   Till all our warfare cease,
And at our Father's loved abode
   Our souls arrive in peace.

230.   C. M.

1 Whence do our mournful thoughts aris
   And where's our courage fled?
Have restless sin and raging hell
   Struck all our comforts dead?

2 Have we forgot the almighty name
   That formed the earth and sea?
And can an all-creating arm
   Grow weary or decay?

3 Treasures of everlasting might
   In our Jehovah dwell;
He gives the conquest to the right,
   And treads their foes to hell.

4 Mere mortal power shall fade and die,
   And youthful vigor cease;
But we that wait upon the Lord
   Shall feel our strength increase.

Confidence and Hope.

231. L. M.

1 Now may the God of power and grace
   Attend his people's humble cry!
Jehovah hears when Israel prays,
   And brings deliverance from on high.

2 The name of Jacob's God defends
   When bucklers fail and brazen walls:
He from his sanctuary sends
   Succor and strength when Zion calls.

3 Well he remembers all our sighs,
   His love exceeds our best deserts;
His love accepts the sacrifice
   Of humble groans and broken hearts.

4 In his salvation is our hope,
   And in the name of Israel's God
Our troops shall lift their banners up,
   Our navies spread their flags abroad.

5 Some trust in horses trained for war,
   And some of chariots make their boasts:
Our surest expectations are
   From thee, the Lord of heavenly hosts.

232. L. M.

1 AFFLICTED land, to Christ draw near,
Thy Saviour's gracious promise hear;
His faithful word declares to thee
That "as thy day, thy strength shall be."

2 Thy faith is weak, thy foes are strong
But if the conflict should be long
Thy Lord will make the foes all flee;
For " as thy day, thy strength shall b[e

3 While persecutions rage and flame,
Still trust in thy Redeemer's name:
In fiery trials thou shalt see
That " as thy day, thy strength shall b[e

4 While called by Him to bear the cros[s
Defeat, disaster, pain, or loss,
Or deep distress, and poverty,
Still " as thy day, thy strength shall b[e

233.   *Ps.* 76—C. M.

1 To God I cried with mournful voi[ce
I sought his gracious ear,
In the sad day when troubles rose
And filled my heart with fear.

2 I called Thy mercies to my mind
Which we enjoyed before;
And will the Lord no more be kin[d
His face appear no more?

3 Will he for ever cast us off?
His promise ever fail?
Has he forgot his tender love?
Shall anger still prevail?

4 Lord, I forbid this hopeless thought,
  This dark, despairing frame,
 Remembering what thy hand hath wrought;
  Thy hand is still the same.

5 When God, in his own sovereign ways,
  Comes down to save the oppressed,
 The wrath of man shall work his praise,
  And he'll restrain the rest.

6 The thunder of his sharp rebuke
  Our haughty foes shall feel;
 For Jacob's God hath not forsook,
  But dwells in Zion still.

234.   *Ps.* 125—S. M.

1 Firm and unmoved are they
  That rest their souls on God;
 Firm as the mount where David dwelt,
  Or where the ark abode.

2 As mountains stood to guard
  The city's sacred ground,
 So God and his almighty love
  Embrace his saints around.

3 What though the Father's rod
  Drop a chastising stroke,
 Yet, lest it wound their souls too deep,
  Its fury shall be broke.

4 Deal gently, Lord, with those
    Whose faith and pious fear,
 Whose hope, and love, and every grace
    Proclaim their hearts sincere.

5 Nor shall the tyrant's rage
    Too long oppress the saint;
The God of Israel will support
    His children, lest they faint.

235.   C. M.

1 HAD not the God of truth and love,
    When hosts against us rose,
Displayed his vengeance from above,
    And crushed the conquering foes,

2 Their armies, like a raging flood,
    Had swept the guardless land;
Destroyed on earth our fair abode,
    And whelmed our feeble band.

3 But safe beneath his spreading shield
    Our sons securely rest,
Defy the dangers of the field,
    And bare the fearless breast.

4 And now our souls shall bless the Lord,
    Who broke the deadly snare;
Who saved us from the murdering sword
    And made our lives his care.

Our help is in Jehovah's name,
  Who formed the heavens above;
He that supports their wondrous frame
  Will still his people love!

36.   8s and 7s.

CALL Jehovah thy Salvation,
  Rest beneath the Almighty's shade,
In his secret habitation
  Dwell, and never be dismayed.

There no tumult shall alarm thee,
  Thou shalt dread no hidden snare;
Guile nor violence can harm thee;
  An eternal safeguard there.

From the sword at noonday wasting,
  From the noisome pestilence,
In the depth of midnight blasting,
  God shall be thy sure defence.

Fear thou not the deadly quiver,
  When a thousand feel the blow,
Mercy shall thy soul deliver,
  Though ten thousand be laid low.

Since, with pure and firm affection,
  Thou on God hast set thy love,
With the wings of his protection
  He will shield thee from above.

237. L. M.

The Officer's Hymn.

1 Mercy and judgment are my song;
And, since they both to thee belong,
My gracious God, my righteous King,
To thee my songs and vows I bring.

2 When I am raised to bear the sword,
I'll take my counsel from thy word;
Thy justice and thy heavenly grace
Shall be the pattern of my ways.

3 Let wisdom all my actions guide,
And let my God with me reside:
No wicked thing shall dwell with me,
Which may provoke thy jealousy.

4 I'll search the land, and raise the just
To posts of honor, wealth, and trust:
The men that work thy holy will
Shall be my friends and favorites still.

5 In vain shall sinners hope to rise
By flattering or malicious lies;
Nor, while the innocent I guard,
Shall bold offenders e'er be spared.

---

* When Washington took command he caused this psalm to be sung during religious service in the presence of the army.

238.   8s and 7s.

1 God shall charge his angel legions
   Watch and ward o'er thee to keep;
Though thou walk through hostile re-
      gions,
   Though in desert wilds thou sleep.

2 On the lion vainly roaring,
   On his young thy foot shall tread;
And, the dragon's den exploring,
   Thou shalt bruise the serpent's head

3 Since, with pure and firm affection,
   Thou on God hast set thy love,
With the wings of his protection
   He will shield thee from above.

4 Thou shalt call on him in trouble,
   He will hearken, he will save;
Here for grief reward thee double,
   Crown with life beyond the grave.

239.   L. M.

1 How long has God bestowed his care
   On this indulged, ungrateful land!
How oft, in times of danger near,
   Preserved us by his sovereign hand!

2 Here peace and liberty have dwelt,
    The glorious gospel brightly shone;
And oft our mightiest foes have felt
    That God has made our cause his own

3 But, ah! both heaven and earth have heard
    Our vile requital of his love;
We, whom like children he has reared,
    For all his care unthankful prove.

4 See; he uplifts his chastening rod!
    O where are now the faithful few
Who tremble for the ark of God,
    And know what Israel ought to do?

5 Lord! hear thy people everywhere,
    Who meet this day to weep and pray
Our sinful land in mercy spare,
    In mercy turn thy wrath away!

240.   C. M.

1 LORD, while for all mankind we pray,
    Of every clime and coast,
O hear us for our native land—
    The land we love the most.

O guard our shores from every foe,
    With peace our borders bless,
2 With prosperous times our cities crown
    Our fields with plenteousness.

Confession, and Humiliation.

3 Unite us in the sacred love
   Of knowledge, truth, and thee;
 And let our hills and valleys shout
   The songs of liberty.

4 Lord of the nations, thus to thee
   Our country we commend;
 Be thou her refuge and her trust,
   Her everlasting friend.

241. C. M.

1 See, gracious God, before thy throne
   Thy mourning people bend!
 'T is on thy sovereign grace alone
   Our humble hopes depend.

2 Tremendous judgments from thy hand
   Thy dreadful power display;
 Yet mercy spares this guilty land,
   And still we live to pray.

3 How changed, alas! are truths divine
   For error, guilt, and shame!
 What impious numbers, bold in sin,
   Disgrace the Christian name!

4 O turn us, turn us, mighty Lord,
   By thy resistless grace;
 Then shall our hearts obey thy word,
   And humbly seek thy face.

5 Thus, though insulting foes invade,
   We will not sink in fear;
Secure of never failing aid,
   If God, our God, is near.

242.   6s and 4s.

1 GOD bless our native land;
Firm may she ever stand
     Through storm and night
When the wild tempests rave,
Ruler of winds and wave,
Do thou our country save,
     By thy great might.

2 For her our prayers shall rise
To God above the skies;
     On him we wait;
Thou who hast heard each sigh,
Watching each weeping eye,
Be thou for ever nigh;
     God save our state.

243.   *Air—*"God save the King."

1 OUR dearly cherished land,
Home of a faithful band,
     For thee we live;
For our homes' purity,
For thy sweet liberty,
For freedom's victory,
     Our *all* we give

Confession, and Humiliation. 233

2 Our fathers, husbands dear,
  Our brothers, lovers near,
    We offer thee;
  While our fond hearts are riven,
  Our prayers ascend to heaven,
  That strength to them be given,
    And victory.

3 Our loved Confederacy,
  May God remember thee,
    And warfare stay.
  May he lift up his hand,
  And smite the oppressor's band,
  While our true patriots stand
    With bravery.

4 To God let voices raise
  Their sweetest songs of praise—
    Proclaim him King.
  When peace o'erspreads our land,
  And we 're a happy band,
  O let each humble hand
    Some offering bring.

244.   L. M.

1 O Lord of Hosts, to thee we kneel,
  To thee amid this strife appeal;
  Forgive our sins against thy laws,
  Against our foes defend our cause.

2 God of our fathers, let thy might
Uphold the truth, support the right;
Be thou our leader, thou our shield,
On each ensanguined battle-field.

3 O thou, most mighty, gird thy sword
Upon thy thigh and give the word,
Now let the flaming pillar guide
Our armies through the battle's tide.

4 Inspire our heroes for the fight,
Spirit of justice, truth, and right;
Then, when the invading hosts shall flee,
A country's thanks shall rise to thee.

245.   L. M.

1 To thee our fathers, Lord, repaired
   In troublous times, and sought relief,
They, mid revengeful foes, were spared,
   And found in thee, joy, ev'n in grief.

2 May we, their children, now oppressed
   By deadly foes and anxious fears,
In thee, our fathers' God, find rest,
   Until deliverance appears.

3 Their faith from thee may we obtain,
   Sustained by hope and peace divine,
While we those liberties maintain
   Which life and treasure far outshine.

Humbly we own unworthiness,
 Confess our sin and guilt with shame,
Trust in the Lord, our righteousness,
 And plead His gracious, glorious name.

Not through our wisdom, nor our strength,
 Not through our leaders, nor our hosts,
But through thy grace, we hope at length
 To echo triumph round our coasts.

16.   S. M.

1 AND will the God of grace
 Perpetual silence keep?
The God of Justice hold his peace,
 And let his vengeance sleep?

2 Behold what cruel snares
 Our faithless foes have spread;
The men that hate thy word and thee,
 Lift up their threatening head.

3 Against thy peaceful sons,
 Their counsels they employ;
And malice, with her watchful eye,
 Pursues them to destroy.

4 Awake, almighty God,
 And call thy power to mind,
Make them to bow beneath thy will,
 While they thy pardon find.

5 Restrain their madness, Lord,
 Lead them to seek thy name;
Or else their impious rage confound,
 And turn their pride to shame.

6 Then shall the nations know
 The just and dreadful God;
Submissive to thy sceptre bow;
 And own thee sovereign Lord.

247.   7s and 6s.

1 My country! O my country!
 My soul with grief is stirred,
As from thy border to thy coast
 The din of war is heard!
And though the victory oft is ours,
 When booming cannons roar;
The widow's moan, the orphan's wail,
 Rise when the strife is o'er!

2 My country! O my country!
 Thy pride hath brought thee low,
But, oh! may righteousness exalt,
 And save thee from thy woe!
Thou wert of him unmindful,
 Whose arm was thy defence,
Till justly he withdrew his aid,
 And showed thine impotence.

My country! O my country!
  Kneel low before thy God,
And humbly pray that he may now
  Remove his chastening rod;
Confess thy sins to Heaven;
  With deep repentance mourn;
And when abased in dust we lie,
  His favor may return.

My country! O my country!
  May God remember thee!
And in his pardoning love avert
  The ills we can not flee;
May he, our only helper,
  Become our future guide,
And we the people of his choice,
  Who in his love abide.

18.   8s and 7s.

Dread Jehovah! God of nations!
  From thy temple in the skies,
Hear thy people's supplications
  Now for their deliverance rise.

Lo! with deep contrition turning,
  Humbly at thy feet we bend;
Hear us, fasting, praying, mourning,
  Hear us, spare us, and defend.

3 Though our sins, our hearts confounding,
    Long and loud for vengeance call,
  Thou hast mercy more abounding;
    Jesus' blood can cleanse them all.

4 Let that love veil our transgression,
    Let that blood our guilt efface:
  Save thy people from oppression,
    Save from spoil thy chosen race.

249.   L. M.

1 While, Lord, our souls thy grace adore
    May Jesus plead our humble claim;
  And thy protection still secure
    Through his prevailing, glorious name

2 With all the boasted pomp of war,
    In vain we dare the hostile field:
  In vain, unless the Lord be there;
    Thine arm alone our country's shield.

3 Let past experience of thy care
    Support our hope, our trust invite!
  Again attend our humble prayer,
    Again be mercy thy delight!

4 Our arms succeed, our councils guide,
    Let thy right hand our cause maintain
  'Till war's destructive rage subside,
    And peace resume her gentle reign.

Confession, and Humiliation.

5 O when shall time the period bring
  When raging war shall waste no more;
When peace shall stretch her balmy wing
From sea to sea, from shore to shore?

250. *Psalm. 6s.*

1 PRAISED be the Lord of might,
  Our rock in all alarms;
By whom we 're taught to fight,
  And triumph through our arms.
Thy heavenly help extend,
  In this our time of woe;
Our lives thy power defend
  From our blood-thirsty foe.

2 Lord, bend the arched skies,
  On wings of wind come down,
And make fierce storms arise,
  And blast them with thy frown;
Bright flames from out the sky,
  Lord, let thy power command,
And let thine arrows fly,
  And drive them from our land.

3 Then in glad songs to thee,
  Will we exalt our voice,
And our blest land be free,
  And in our God rejoice.

Thrice happy, Lord, are they
  On whom such blessings fall!
Thrice blessed, blessed they!
  Whom thou thy people call.

251.   C. M.

1 Lord, thou hast scourged our bleedin
    land;
  Behold thy people mourn;
Shall vengeance always rule thy hand?
  Shall mercy ne'er return?

2 Our country trembles at the stroke;
  Avert thy lifted hand;
Thy gracious presence we invoke,
  To save the stricken land.

3 Exalt Thy banner in the field,
  For those that fear thy name;
From vengeful hosts our nation shield,
  And put our foes to shame.

4 Attend our armies to the fight,
  And be their guardian God;
In vain shall numerous hosts unite
  Against thy lifted rod.

5 Our troops beneath thy guiding hand,
  Shall gain a glad renown:
'T is God who makes the feeble stand,
  And treads the mighty down.

Confession, and Humiliation.

152. C. M.

1 Lord, look on all assembled here,
    Who in thy presence stand,
To offer up united prayer
    For this our sinful land.

2 O may we all, with one consent,
    Fall low before thy throne,
With tears the nation's sins lament,
    The Church's, and our own.

3 And should the dread decree be past,
    And we still feel the rod—
Let faith and patience hold us fast
    To our correcting God.

53. S. M.

1 Jesus, who knows full well
    The heart of every saint,
Invites us all our griefs to tell,
    To pray and never faint.

2 He bows his gracious ear,
    We never plead in vain:
Yet we must wait till he appear,
    And pray, and pray again.

3 Jesus the Lord will hear
    His chosen when they cry,
Yes, though he may a while forbear,
    He'll help them from on high.

4 His nature, truth, and love,
    Engage him on our side;
When we are grieved his bowels move,
    And can we be denied?

5 Then let us earnest be,
    And never faint in prayer;
He loves our importunity,
    And makes our cause his care.

254. S. M.

1 Mourn for the thousands slain,
    The youthful and the strong;
Mourn for the wine-cup's fatal reign,
    And the deluded throng.

2 Mourn for the ruined soul—
    Eternal life and light—
Lost by the fiery, maddening bowl,
    And turned to hopeless night.

3 Mourn for the lost—but call—
    Call to the strong—the free;
Rouse them to shun that dreadful fall,
    And to the refuge flee.

4 Mourn for the lost—but pray—
    Pray to our God above,
To break the fell destroyer's sway,
    And show his saving love.

255. C. M.

1 When Abrah'm, full of sacred awe,
    Before Jehovah stood,
  And with a humble, fervent prayer,
    For guilty Sodom sued:

2 With what success, what wondrous grace,
    Was his petition crowned!
  The Lord would spare, if in the place
    Ten righteous men were found.

3 And could a single pious soul
    So rich a boon obtain,
  Great God, and shall a nation cry,
    And plead with thee in vain?

4 Are not the righteous dear to thee
    Now, as in ancient times?
  Or does this sinful land exceed
    Gomorrah in her crimes?

5 Still we are thine: we bear thy name;
    Here yet is thine abode;
  Long has thy presence blessed our land;
    Forsake us not, O God.

256. L. M.

1 On thee, O Lord our God, we call,
  Before thy throne devoutly fall;
  O whither should the helpless fly?
  To whom but thee direct their cry?

2 Lord, we repent, we weep, we mourn,
To our forsaken God we turn;
O spare our bleeding country, spare—
Is not her cause to thee most dear?

3 We plead thy grace, indulgent God;
We plead thy Son's atoning blood;
We plead thy gracious promises;
And are these unavailing pleas?

4 These pleas, presented at thy throne,
Have brought ten thousand blessings down
On guilty lands in helpless woe;
Let them prevail to save us too.

257. C. M.

1 Behold us, Lord, and let our cry
　　Before thy throne ascend;
Cast thou on us a pitying eye,
　　And still our lives defend.

2 For impious foes insult us round;
　　Oppressive, proud, and vain;
They cast thy temples to the ground,
　　And all our rights profane.

3 Yet thy forgiving grace we trust,
　　And in thy power rejoice;
Thine arms shall bring our foes to dust,
　　Thy praise inspire our voice.

58. L. M.

Look down, O Lord, with pitying eye,
Though loud our crimes for vengeance cry;
Let mercy's louder voice prevail,
Nor thy long suffering patience fail.

O let thy sovereign grace impart
Contrition to each rocky heart;
And bid sincere repentance flow,
In general, undissembled woe.

Fair, smiling peace again restore:
With plenty bless the pining poor;
And may a happy, thankful land,
Obedient own thy guardian hand.

59. L. M.

Great Ruler of the earth and skies,
   A word of thine almighty breath
Can sink the world or bid it rise:
   Thy smile is life, thy frown is death.

When angry nations rush to arms,
   And rage, and noise, and tumult reign,
And war resounds its dire alarms,
   And slaughter dyes the hostile plain—

Thy sov'reign eye looks calmly down,
   And marks their course, and bounds
     their power;
Thy law the angry nations own,
   And wrathful passions rage no more.

4 Then the loud cannon cease to roar,
  And warlike trumps no longer sound
The din of arms is heard no more,
  No human blood pollutes the ground.
5 Let peace return with balmy wing;
  And all thy blessings round her shed!
Glad plenty laugh, the valleys sing,
  Reviving commerce lift her head.
6 To thee we 'll pay our grateful songs;
  Thy kind protection still implore:
And all our hearts, and lives, and tongues
  Confess thy goodness, and adore.

260.   L. M.—6-*Line.*

1 GREAT God, inspire each heart and
    tongue
  Thy wondrous goodness to proclaim;
And bid the animating song
  Glow with devotion's lively flame.
To thee our favored land would raise
Her sweetest notes of thankful praise.
2 But where shall we begin to trace
    The wonders of thy hand divine?
In every season, every place,
    How numerous and how bright they
      shine.
To God our favored land would raise
Her sweetest notes of thankful praise.

Alas! beneath the hostile sword
   Has many a worthy patriot bled,
And many a mourning heart deplored
   A friend, a son, a brother dead!
The sword is sheath'd—O let us raise
To God our sweetest notes of praise.

The horrors of th' ensanguined field,
   Which sadden'd victory's fairest plume,
To scenes of pleasure now shall yield.
   And peace her gentle reign resume.
To God our favored land shall raise
Her sweetest notes of thankful praise.

Crown, gracious God, thy gift of peace
   With gifts yet nobler, more divine!
O let thy all-prevailing grace
   On our dear land with glory shine!
Devotion then to thee shall raise
Sublimer notes of thankful praise.

261.   L. M.

Thine earthly Sabbath, Lord, we love;
But there 's a nobler rest above;
To that our lab'ring souls aspire,
With ardent pangs of strong desire.

No more fatigue, no more distress;
Nor sin, nor hell shall reach the place;
No sighs shall mingle with the songs
Which warble from immortal tongues.

3 No rude alarms of raging foes,
   No cares to break the long repose,
   No midnight shade, no clouded sun,
   But sacred, high, eternal noon.

4 O long expected day, begin;
   Dawn on these realms of woe and sin;
   Fain would we leave this weary road,
   And sleep in death, to rest with God.

262. L. M.

1 The billows swell, the winds are high;
   Clouds overcast my wintry sky:
   Out of the depths to thee I call;
   My fears are great, my strength is small.

2 O Lord, the pilot's part perform,
   And guide and guard me through the storm;
   Defend me from each threatening ill:
   Control the waves; say "Peace! be still."

3 Amid the roaring of the sea
   My soul still hangs her hope on thee;
   Thy constant love, thy faithful care,
   Are all that save me from despair.

4 Though tempest-tossed, and half a wreck,
   My Saviour through the floods I seek:
   Let neither winds nor stormy main
   Force back my shattered bark again.

263.   L. M.

1 WHEN marshalled on the nightly plain,
   The glittering hosts bestud the sky,
One star alone, of all the train,
   Can fix the sinner's wandering eye.

2 Hark! hark! to God the chorus breaks
   From every host, from every gem;
But one alone, the Saviour speaks:
   It is the Star of Bethlehem.

3 Once on the raging seas I rode,
   The storm was loud, the night was dark;
The ocean yawned, and rudely blowed
   The wind that tossed my foundering bark.

4 Deep horror then my vitals froze;
   Death-struck, I ceased the tide to stem:
When suddenly a star arose!
   It was the Star of Bethlehem.

5 It was my guide, my light, my all;
   It bade my dark forebodings cease;
And, through the storm, and danger's thrall,
   It led me to the port of peace.

6 Now safely moored, my perils o'er,
   I 'll sing, first in night's diadem,
For ever and for evermore,
   The Star—the Star of Bethlehem!

264. C. M.

1 How are thy servants blessed, O Lord
   How sure is their defence!
Eternal wisdom is their guide,
   Their help Omnipotence.

2 In foreign realms, and lands remote,
   Supported by thy care;
Thro' burning climes they pass unhurt,
   And breathe in tainted air.

3 When by the dreadful tempest borne
   High on the broken wave,
They know thou art not slow to hear,
   Nor impotent to save.

4 The storm is laid—the winds retire,
   Obedient to thy will;
The sea that roars at thy command,
   At thy command is still.

5 In midst of dangers, fears, and deaths,
   Thy goodness we 'll adore;
We 'll praise thee for thy mercies past,
   And humbly hope for more.

6 Our life, while thou preserv'st that life,
   Thy sacrifice shall be;
And death, when death shall be our lot,
   Shall join our souls to thee.

265.   8s and 7s.

1 TOSSED upon life's raging billow,
   Sweet it is, O Lord, to know
Thou didst press a sailor's pillow,
   And canst feel a sailor's woe.

2 Never slumbering, never sleeping,
   Though the night be dark and drear,
Thou the faithful watch art keeping:
   "All, all 's well," thy constant cheer.

And, though loud the wind is howling,
   Fierce though flash the lightnings red,
Darkly though the storm-cloud 's scowling
   O'er the sailor's anxious head—

Thou canst calm the raging ocean,
   All its noise and tumult still;
Hush the tempest's wild commotion,
   At the bidding of thy will.

Thus my heart the hope will cherish,
   While to thee I lift mine eye:
Thou wilt save me ere I perish,
   Thou wilt hear the sailor's cry.

6 And, though mast and sail be riven,
  Soon life's voyage will be o'er;
Safely moor'd in heaven's wide haven,
  Storm and tempest vex no more.

266.   12s.

1 When through the torn sail the wild tempest is streaming,
When o'er the dark wave the red lightning is gleaming,
Nor hope lends a ray the poor seaman to cherish,
We fly to our Maker: help, Lord, or we perish!

2 O Jesus, once tossed on the breast of the billow,
Aroused by the shriek of despair from thy pillow,
Now seated in glory, the mariner cherish,
Who cries in his danger, "Help, Lord, or we perish!"

3 And oh! when the whirlwind of passion is raging,
When hell in our hearts its wild warfare is waging,
Arise in thy strength, thy redeemed to cherish!
Rebuke the destroyer—help, Lord, or we perish!

267
7s and 6s.

1 Though hard the winds are blowing,
  And loud the billows roar;
Full swiftly we are going
  To our dear native shore.

2 The billows breaking o'er us,
  The storms that round us swell,
Are aiding to restore us
  To all we loved so well.

3 So sorrow often presses
  Life's mariner along;
Afflictions and distresses
  Are gales and billows strong.

4 The sharper and severer
  The storms of life we meet,
The sooner and the nearer
  Is heaven's eternal seat.

5 Come, then, afflictions dreary,
  Sharp sickness, pierce my breast;
You only bear the weary
  More quickly home to rest.

268.
6s.

1 When many a tempest blew,
  And hope was almost past,
The worn and weary crew
  Hail'd distant land at last.

2 Far o'er the lee it lay,
    Its arms seem'd spreading wide,
 To form a quiet bay,
    Where ships might safely ride.

3 That refuge from the storm,
    That distant bay so fair,
 Was but a cloudy form,
    And melted into air!

4 So earthly hope deceives
    The heart that trusts it most;
 So all the beauty leaves
    Some seeming happy coast.

5 But faith can look before,
    And see the land of light;
 That is the only shore
    That never mocks the sight.

269.   C. M.

1 Blest be that voice now heard afar
    O'er the dark, rolling sea,
 That whispers to the hardy tar,
    "Sailor, there's hope for thee!"

2 Blest be that pure, that Christian love,
    That boundless charity,
 Which bears the olive, like the dove,
    Brave, generous tar, to thee.

Blest be those lips, in accents mild,
 From sordid motives free,
That first proclaimed to ocean's child,
 " Sailor, there 's hope for thee."
Long hadst thou rode the foamy wave,
 From sin nor danger free,
Till mercy stretch'd her arm to save—
 To save, brave sailor, thee.
God of the just! O lend thine ear,
 And blessings rich decree
On those who spread these tidings dear—
 " Sailor, there 's hope for thee!"

70.   C. M.
How sweet the songs of Zion sound
 When seamen tune their voice
In praise to him who reigns on high,
 And bids the world rejoice.
Those tongues, which once their God
  blasphemed,
 Now sound his praises high
For that sweet word of gospel grace
 Which brings a Saviour nigh.
They sing, to tell how God has given
 Deliverance from the storm,
And brought them to their port in peace
 By his most gracious arm.

4 They sing, to tell of all the love
   Of him who died to save;
 Who now in glory reigns above.
   To rescue from the grave.

5 Sing on, dear seamen, sing and tell
   Of all Emmanuel's love!
 And may you rise and sit on high,
   And reign with him above.

271. C. M.

1 When o'er the mighty deep we rode,
   By winds and storms assail'd;
 We call'd upon the ocean's God,
   Whose mercy never fail'd.

2 The raging tempest heard thy voice,
   The winds obey'd thy will;
 The elements withheld their noise,
   And all the floods were still.

3 With joy we hail'd the distant shore,
   And safe the vessel moor'd:
 With grateful hearts, that happy hour,
   We praised the ocean's Lord.

4 And when life's voyage too is past,
   And we are call'd to die,
 O may we see thy face at last,
   In realms beyond the sky.

www.ingramcontent.com/pod-product-compliance
Lightning Source LLC
Chambersburg PA
CBHW021401230426
43666CB00006B/604